FRESHWATER
FISHING
PROPERLY
EXPLAINED

Ian Ball

RIGHT WAY

Printed and bound in Great Britain by Cox & Wyman Ltd., Reading,
Berkshire.

The *Right Way* series is published by Elliot Right Way Books,
Brighton Road, Lower Kingswood, Tadworth, Surrey, KT20 6TD,
U.K.

CONTENTS

ACKNOWLEDGMENTS

My thanks to Jim Lester and W. E. (Bill) Davies for their lovely line drawings which enhance these pages.

1

QUICK QUIZ QUESTIONS

1. Was the first published book about fishing written by a woman, or a man?
   Answer on page 9.
2. Can fish speak?
   Answer on page 12.
3. Describe the food chain.
   Answer on page 14.
4. What action should be taken immediately if you think you've landed a record breaking fish?
   Answer on page 16.
5. What is a barbule?
   Answer on page 18.
6. Do eels breed in freshwater?
   Answer on page 27.
7. When did zander come to the U.K.?
   Answer on page 39.
8. How may we best breed maggots?
   Answer on page 48.
9. When might you need a "double grinner"?
   Answer on page 56.
10. Why should you wet your hands before touching a fish?
    Answer on page 67.
11. What are the main aims of groundbaiting?
    Answer on page 68.
12. If you were "stret-pegging", what would you be doing?
    Answer on page 84.
13. Give 2 advantages legering can have over other methods of fishing.
    Answer on page 86.
14. Name 5 advantages of Pole fishing over angling with rod and line.
    Answer on page 93.

15. What is a "peg"?
    Answer on page 95.
16. NYMPH, DUN, SPENT SPINNER. What are they?
    Answer on page 98.
17. Which colour spinning lures generally catch most fish?
    Answer on page 108.
18. List 12 locations in flowing water likely to hold big trout.
    Answer on page 109.
19. What useful information should be recorded in our fishing records?
    Answer on page 114.
20. What is a "put-and-take" fishery?
    Answer on page 117.
21. List five advantages of joining a fishing club.
    Answer on page 122.

2

YOU ARE A HUNTER

You are a hunter. So am I. We understand each other. Come with me; let us explore the sport of freshwater fishing and share the thrill and excitement of hunting and catching fish.

"And if I follow," you ask. "Can I become a catcher of big fish?"

"Yes, you should. I promise."

Beginner or expert, you'll learn from and enjoy this up-to-date book.

Man has hunted fish for food and sport for 2 million years. People have fished with rod, line and hook for at least 20,000 years.

Escape from your worries into the timeless sport of fishing magic, mystery and challenge.

Read these pages and discover the charm and desire that drew our ancestors to the relaxing silence of the water's edge in pursuit of fish.

At one with nature

Young and old, we can all unwind and feel at one with nature while fishing. Away from machine noise and crowd bustle we find peace and happiness by the water. And we are never alone. Look round and enjoy the bright colours of kingfishers, butterflies and dragonflies. Smell the sweet perfume of flowers and grasses. Stare into the rippling waters; spot minnows, waterboatmen, beetles, crawling crayfish, ramshorn snails and rich growths of water plants like hornwort and willow moss. Check soft earth for prints of badger, fox, hare and vole.

The spell cast over us on a misty summer's morning or crackling-white, frosty winter's day, is the same bewitching enchantment felt by freshwater fishermen of ancient times.

We no longer need to hunt fish for food, but we still get that age-old thrill of excitement and pleasure at catching a fish.

1. The River Till, Northumberland.

You are born a hunter!

Fishing is your kind of sport
You can choose to fish on your own; with your family, or a club. You may decide to use basic, inexpensive equipment or invest in the best quality tackle you can afford. You might spend a day fishing in one place, or an hour or two moving along the waterside.

Fishing is *your* sport and you may fish the way that gives you most joy and satisfaction.

A warm welcome to women
Women have always fished and today many more women are starting in the sport. The first fishing book ever published, "The Treatyse of Fyshinge wyth an Angle" (1496) was written by a woman, Dame Juliana Berners. She may have written the book 50 years before it was published. Izaac Walton's famous book, "The Compleat Angler" was not published until 1653 – 157 years after Dame Juliana's book! Walton's book is still printed and available in hardback and paperback editions.

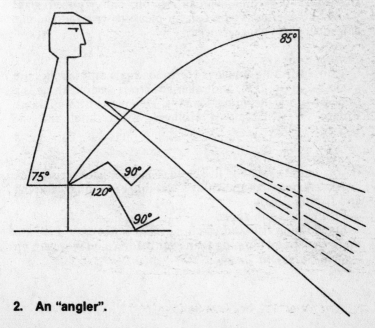

2. **An "angler".**

An angler

As you see from the sketch on page 9, fishing is all angles. The name "angler" has been used in the U.K. for several hundred years and perhaps it is because when we fish, our rod and line forms an angle. We are "angling" for fish. The name *angler* also shows we are not fishermen using nets.

Coarse fishermen

Some people who fish with rod and line prefer to call themselves fishermen. A *coarse* angler or fisherman fishes for coarse fish. All freshwater fish except salmon and trout are "coarse" fish. Salmon and trout are called *game* fish because they are wise and strong fighting fish, offering us good "game" or sport.

Nobody knows for sure why most freshwater fish are called coarse fish. Some say the reason is their coarse flavour when cooked; others believe the name comes from the coarse, rough scales on the skin of many freshwater fish, compared to the smoother scales of the game fish – salmon and trout. In America, "coarse" fish are called "rough" fish.

Your guess is as good as anyone's. Angler, coarse angler, freshwater fisherman/woman/person; call yourself what you will. Americans who fish for pleasure with rod and line call themselves *sport fishers*.

Fishing holidays

Organised fishing holidays for individuals and families are available in the U.K. and other countries where fishing is a popular sport, including: Canada, Denmark, Eire, Finland, France, West Germany, Holland, Switzerland and the U.S.A.

Camp it

If you want to fish and live close to nature, pack a rucksack or bicycle panniers and enjoy a walking or cycling, camping and fishing holiday.

Fishing is a fun sport.

But hunting fish and catching them is not easy. Fish are more clever and cunning than ever before. Today we are up against *Superfish*.

3

SUPERFISH

Fish have learned a lot about us over the last couple of million years. Prehistoric man, Ancient Egyptians, Greeks and Romans have painted pictures of themselves fishing. We've all shared the same problems: where are the big fish; how can we get near them undetected; what's the best bait to use, and how should we land our fish once hooked?

More fish get off the hook than are caught. We have much to learn.

Big brainy fish
Big fish are clever. They only live to grow big by being smart. You have to get up early in the morning to fool them.

Fish know we are hunters and keep an eye on our latest baits, tackle and methods. With more of us starting fishing for sport, fish have extra practice avoiding our hooks.

Modern research has shown that big fish educate baby fish and we have to think of new ways to catch them. Wise fish outwit us; grow huge (for their species) and pass their secrets to young fish. This is what we are up against – big brainy fish.

Fish ears
Beware! Fish have ears. Sound is clearer in water than in air. Fish have ears inside the head and hear us coming from as far away as 12 m (40 feet) in any direction. We must sneak down on them.

Fishy smell
Fish have a highly-developed sense of smell. They track food for long distances in muddy water and at night. Fish are also able to detect tiny traces of chemicals in water and are upset by the slightest pollution.

Fish eyes
Fish have all round, full-colour daytime sight. They see

everything happening around them without moving their bodies. At night and in murky water fish switch to black and white vision. Fish have no eyelids and sleep with eyes open.

Water acts like a mirror and fish see any movement in the water reflected on the underneath of the surface. Fish also spot motion on the bank and at the water's edge.

Touch and taste

A fish knows when the water temperature alters by a fraction of a degree.

Fish do not need to take food into their mouths to taste. Fish can taste food just by touching it with their lips. Hooks in bait may be felt and the bait rejected, or simply sucked off the hook.

Fish wear combat jackets

Fish are camouflaged by colour patterns which blend in with their surroundings – just as we wear clothes for fishing that make us difficult for fish to see. Fish are hard to find by glancing into the water, because they swim in "camouflaged combat jackets". Fish are white underneath and invisible to an enemy below, who can't see them because the fish's belly matches the sky. The white belly gives a flashing effect when hooked fish roll to dislodge a hook.

Fish speak

Yes, fish talk to each other in "fishese". They pass information and gossip through the water in secret code about food, natural enemies and fishermen, by moving their bodies and insides to make special sounds only they understand. And if the message to scoot is broadcast, fish move fast. A 457 mm (18 inch) fish sprints at about 16 miles per hour and cruises at 10 miles per hour.

So, how can we hope to catch *Superfish*? Well, we can, read on . . .

3. Superfish.

4

FOOD CHAIN

Our hunt for fish begins with a look at the way their food develops in fresh water. Knowing what fish eat gives clues to help us catch big fish.

Life-giving plants
Plants of various sizes grow in fresh water. Some large plants root and rise from the bottom, while others grow and flourish near the surface. Microscopic plants float on top of water. Life in fresh water depends on plants.

Plants draw energy from the sun's rays and convert sunlight into life-giving oxygen, which they bubble into the water.

Plants clean water by filtering waste matter passed out by fish and insects and convert the waste into nourishing nutrients like nitrogen and phosphates that help plants grow. All dead things are broken down by bacteria into nutrients to be used by plants.

Plants provide fish with food, supply shelter from strong sunlight and offer a hiding place from enemies – kingfishers, herons, otters and big fish who eat smaller fish. Plants also give fish somewhere to lay their eggs.

Fish, snails, shrimps, insects, worms and many other forms of freshwater life feed on plants.

All types of water life are eaten by fish.

Food chain
This story links into a chain of events that goes full circle.

Plants and microscopic water insects are eaten by large insects that are swallowed by small fish, which are eaten by bigger fish, who are gobbled up by great fish.

We must remember the importance of water plants to the food chain when we go fishing. Where we see plants, we know there will be fish!

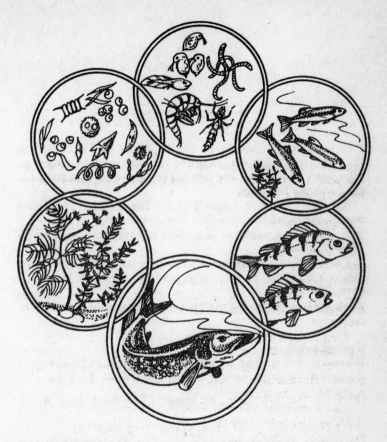

4.   The food chain.

5

FISH FILE

Pick your fish before you go fishing. Study the "Fish file" on the next few pages; decide which fish you want to catch and then read on to find the top tackle and best methods for catching the big ones.

All our fish have English and Latin names. The Latin names are used by scientists of every nation. In the "Fish file", the Latin name of each fish is bracketed next to its English name.

Fish belong to families and fish belonging to the same family are related to each other, even though they may look very different.

REMEMBER: *to know your fish helps you plan how best to catch him.*

Record breakers
When you hook a fish big enough to be a record breaker (see *Record rod-caught weight* in the "Fish file") TRY to:

(a) Keep the fish alive (an angler's fine-mesh *keep net* is ideal).
(b) Take several good photographs (see page 67).
(c) Gather as many witnesses as you are able (note names, addresses and telephone numbers).
(d) Weigh the fish in front of the witnesses on an accurate spring-balance or scales as soon as possible (see page 67).
(e) Immediately 'phone your local specialist tackle dealer and/or a national angling newspaper or magazine. Keep a note of special "hotline" telephone numbers for record claims – see angling press for details.

Politely ask a "witness" to 'phone on your behalf while you nurse the celebrity fish. Await advice and instructions from the experts contacted by telephone.

And support your local newspaper by contacting the editor with your front page "scoop" story.

But the fish comes first
Should the fish appear to be suffering, make do with your photographs and the names, addresses and 'phone numbers of witnesses, and release your fish to recover fully in the safe and secure atmosphere of its water.

Stop Press
Information given in your "Fish file" is correct at the moment of printing. Our knowledge of fish behaviour is constantly advanced by anglers' painstaking observation, reasoning and accurate record keeping (see Chapter 22) – enabling us to go out and catch big record breaking specimen fish!

Up-date facts about fish by regularly reading angling newspapers and magazines.

Sport **** Star **** Ratings
Each species of fish in your "Fish file" is star rated to give an idea of the fish's usual fighting and sporting qualities. You might disagree with my ratings after you've fought with the fish, in which case please amend the ratings and award or take away a *Star*.

BARBEL

Name: Barbel (Barbus barbus).
Family: Cyprinidae. Other members of family found in Europe, Africa and Asia.
Record rod-caught weight: 7 Kg 314 g (16 lbs 2 oz).
Place caught: River Medway, Kent (1994).
Caught by: P. Woodhouse.
Size we can expect to catch: Average weight about 1.81 Kg (4 lbs).
Where barbel like to live: On the bottom of fast flowing streams and rivers. Found in many rivers, especially the Hampshire Avon, Dorset Stour, Kennet, Lea, Nidd, Severn, Swale, Thames, Trent, Welland, Ure and Yorkshire Ouse. Barbel are spreading fast, assisted by angling Clubs introducing barbel to Club waters.

5. Barbel.

How to recognise barbel: Long snout with 4 barbules (feelers) on thick lipped, drooping mouth. Green-brown back, pink-orange fins and silver-white belly.

Sport "Star" rating: ******Excellent fighting fish******

Barbel's favourite natural food: Worms, insects, small fish and water plants.

Baits to catch barbel: Bread flake, bread paste, caddis grubs, cheese paste, hempseed, luncheon meat, maggots, sausage (lightly boiled), silkweed, slugs, wasp grubs, worms.

Barbel's peak sporting fitness: AUGUST/SEPTEMBER/OCTOBER/NOVEMBER/DECEMBER/JANUARY/FEBRUARY.

Know your barbel: Barbel is known as "Old Whiskers" to his friends, who say barbel should visit the barbus for a shave. Barbel (Barbus barbus) is a powerful fish who always gives us a fight to remember.

Barbel grow big and a few probably reach 9 Kg (20 lbs). But such huge barbel are clever and have not been caught in the U.K. A barbel of 7 Kg 260 g (16 lbs 1 oz) was accidentally hooked in the fin and landed by C. H. Cassey in 1960 on the Hampshire Avon at Ibsley. Because the barbel was hooked in its fin and therefore not caught fairly (hooked in the lip) it was not counted as a record.

Barbel use the feelers on their mouths to find food amongst plants, stones, roots and mud.

Barbel swim in shoals, usually hugging the river bed. They hide in holes and deep pools beside weirs or dams and in water plants or submerged tree roots. Barbel are shy, moody fish and sometimes sulk for days without feeding. When barbel feed they hungrily wolf down food and stick to regular mealtimes. Some shoals of barbel feed only in one spot.

Big Barbus barbus is waiting for you!

Groundbait effective? YES – see Chapter 12.

Best fishing methods for BIG Barbel: Legering (see Chapter 15) and float fishing (see Chapter 14).

Right line strength for big barbel: At least 2.26 Kg (5 lbs) breaking strain.

BREAM

Name: Bream, bronze (Abramis brama).

Family: Cyprinidae. Other members of family found in Europe, Africa and Asia.

Record rod-caught weight: 7 Kg 512 g (16 lbs 9 oz).

Place caught: Syndicate (secret) Water, S. England (1991).

Caught by: M. McKeown.

Size we can expect to catch: Average weight about 1.36 Kg (3 lbs).

Where bream like to live: On the bottom of deep, quiet, slow-moving or still waters. Common in canals, lakes, lochs, ponds, reservoirs and rivers across the U.K., notably: The Cheshire meres, Great Ouse, Nene, Norfolk Broads, Severn, Thames, Welland, Witham, Yorkshire Ouse etc.

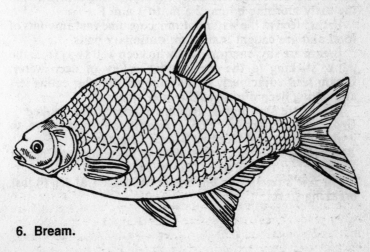

6. Bream.

How to recognise bream: When young silvery; adult bream bronze-brown; wide-bodied, hump-backed. Tail fin deep forked.

Sport "Star" rating: **** Good fighting fish ****.

Bream's favourite natural food: Insects, shellfish, vegetable matter, worms.

Baits to catch bream: Bread flake, bread paste, maggots, worms.

Bream's peak sporting fitness: AUGUST/SEPTEMBER/OCTOBER/NOVEMBER/DECEMBER/JANUARY/FEBRUARY/MARCH.

Know your bream: Bream is a disciplined and orderly shoal fish. New born bream congregate in shoals 100's, sometimes 1,000's, strong. Each shoal is gradually reduced in numbers by natural predators and normal death, until only a few big bream survive. Because bream shoal at birth and probably stay in the same shoal until they die, bream belonging to a particular shoal are all of roughly the same size. Spy one big bream rolling on the surface and you'll know other big bream aren't far away. Every shoal has a leader and he patrols an area of water to a carefully rehearsed time-table, followed closely by his shoal. The bream shoal's predictably regimented pattern of movement and behaviour gives observant fishermen the chance to catch many bream at precise times and locations – whole shoals can be caught by astute anglers. However, really big bream feed at night, or in the early morning hours (2 a.m. to 3 a.m.).

Bream feed at the water bottom; consume vast amounts of food and are caught mainly on stationary baits.

Bream are shy, cautious fish, who keep well away from the bank; sticking to the comparative safety of deep water. Bream feed voraciously in the summer months; eating less and diving deep during cold winter weeks.

Bream are slow but determined fighters once hooked.

Groundbait effective? YES (exceptionally responsive to groundbaiting and "feeding") – see Chapter 12.

Best fishing methods for BIG Bream: Legering (see Chapter 15) and float fishing (see Chapter 14).

Right line strength for big bream: At least 1.81 Kg (4 lbs) breaking strain.

CARP

Name: Carp, common (Cyprinus carpio).
Family: Cyprinidae. Other members of family found in Europe, Africa and Asia.
Record rod-caught weight: 25 Kg 61 g (55 lbs 4 oz).
Place caught: Mid-Northants Fishery (1995).
Caught by: A. White.
Size we can expect to catch: Average weight about 2.72 Kg (6 lbs).
Where carp like to live: Mud-bottomed lakes, rivers, gravel pits and ponds. Carp like quiet, heavily weeded, sluggish water. Many of the really big carp can be found only in Club and private syndicate waters.

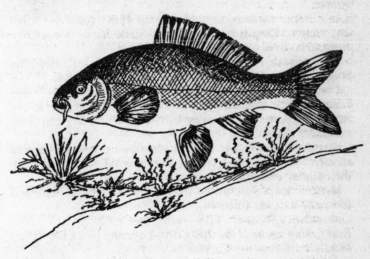

7. Carp.

How to recognise carp: Thick, deep body. Large, greenish-brown scales. Two barbules (feelers) on each side of its upper jaw.
Sport "Star" rating: ****** Excellent fighting fish ******
Carp's favourite natural food: Water plants and vegetable matter; worms, insects and shellfish.
Baits to catch carp: Earthworms, bread paste (mixed with

honey or yeast extract spread); small potatoes – lightly boiled (see page 52), green peas, maggots, wasp grubs, "casters" (see page 48); cheese paste, cherries (stone removed); most types of grain (see page 52); special commercially produced high protein baits; legered floating crust (see page 89), sweetcorn.

Carp's peak sporting fitness: AUGUST/SEPTEMBER/OCTOBER/NOVEMBER/DECEMBER.

Know your carp: Carp is a native of Asia, where he is often bred in "stockponds" as a food fish; they grow huge very quickly. Carp were probably brought to Europe by the Romans, and introduced to the U.K. in the fourteenth century by monks, who kept carp in stockponds; fishing and catching them for the traditional religious Friday fish supper.

In European waters, carp of over 29.48 Kg (65 lbs) are not uncommon. Carp live a long time. Some have, in captivity, lived to be over 40 years old!

They are shy, highly intelligent fish; wary of unfamiliar foods fished as bait, and notoriously difficult to catch.

Carp live alone, or in small groups. They are moody and fickle feeders; affected by light and water temperature; losing interest in particular foods or baits at a whim. Big carp feed mainly at night.

Warm weather brings the best sport; carp tend to become inactive on numerous waters during cold winter months, though they can still be caught.

Hooked carp pull away like trains and fight hard and furiously for their freedom.

Groundbait effective? YES – see Chapter 12.

Best fishing methods for BIG Carp: Legering (see Chapter 15) and float fishing (see Chapter 14).

Right line strength for big carp: At least 3.62 Kg (8 lbs) breaking strain.

CHUB

Name: Chub (Leuciscus cephalus).
Family: Cyprinidae. Other members of family found in Europe, Africa and Asia.
Record rod-caught weight: 3 Kg 743 g (8 lbs 4 oz).

Place caught: River Avon, Christchurch (1913).
Caught by: G.F. Smith.
Size we can expect to catch: Average weight about 680 g (1½ lbs).
Where chub like to live: Prefer flowing water – rivers and streams. Introduced to some stillwaters. Chub are fond of waters like the Dorset Stour, Great Ouse, Hampshire Avon, Kennet, Ribble, Severn, Thames, Trent, Welland and Wye. Chub are not found in most parts of north Scotland, west Wales, Devon or Cornwall.

8. Chub.

How to recognise chub: Big head and mouth, with thick, pale lips. Dark back; large silver/bronze scales. Black edged tail; bright red lower fins.
Sport "Star" rating: **** Good fighting fish ****
Chub's favourite natural food: Small fish, frogs, fruit, insects, shellfish, worms.
Baits to catch chub: Banana cubes, beetles, bluebottles, bread crust, cubes and paste; casters (see page 48), caterpillars, cheese (particularly Danish blue or Gorgonzola), cherries (stone removed), elderberries, hempseed, luncheon meat, macaroni (boiled), maggots, sausage (lightly

boiled), silkweed, slugs, snails, strawberries, sweetcorn, wasp grubs, worms.

Chub's peak sporting fitness: AUGUST/SEPTEMBER/OCTOBER/NOVEMBER/DECEMBER/JANUARY/FEBRUARY.

Know your chub: Chub is a strong, bulky fish with a large appetite. He's a sociable shoal fish, but also inclined to be shy and independent; often leaving the shoal to hunt food on his own – big chub usually choose to live a solitary existence. Chub like underwater holes and hollows; submerged roots and overhanging bushes and trees. Chub feed at all depths; in cold weather chub browse along the water bottom; when the temperature rises, they cruise the surface. Chub feed at any hour of the day or night, and once hooked immediately dive for the safety of obstacles and snags. Because chub are timid, cautious fish, they must be approached extra carefully; or they'll soon disappear from the stretch of water you're fishing. Chub grow BIG. A chub of 4.76 Kg (10 lbs 8 oz) was caught by Dr. J.A. Cameron while fishing the river Annan (Scotland) in 1955. However, the chub was not kept for official verification as a record breaker.

Groundbait effective? YES – see Chapter 12.

Best fishing methods for BIG Chub: Legering (see Chapter 15), float fishing (see Chapter 14), spinning (see Chapter 19) and fly fishing (see Chapter 18).

Right line strength for big chub: At least 2.26 Kg (5 lbs) breaking strain.

DACE

Name: Dace (Leuciscus leuciscus).

Family: Cyprinidae. Other members of family found in Europe, Africa and Asia.

Record rod-caught weight: 574 g (1 lb 4 oz).

Place caught: Little Ouse, Thetford, Norfolk (1960).

Caught by: J. L. Gasson.

Size we can expect to catch: Average weight about 115 g (4 oz).

Where dace like to live: Widespread in England and Wales. Dace like the fast running water of rivers and streams.

9. Dace.

How to recognise dace: Slim, silvery fish. Dark brown or blue-green back. Lower fins yellowish, or soft pink.

Sport "Star" Rating: ***** Very good fighting fish *****

Dace's favourite natural food: Insects, worms and water plants.

Baits to catch dace: Maggots, worms, silkweed, bread crust, flake, paste, hempseed, small berries (especially ripe elderberries).

Dace's peak sporting fitness: SEPTEMBER/OCTOBER/ NOVEMBER/DECEMBER/JANUARY/FEBRUARY/MARCH.

Know your dace: Dace is a gregarious shoal fish. He is always active, frisking, dashing and darting near the surface. Dace feed mainly at the surface and mid-water in warm weather, preferring the water bottom during cold periods. "Dainty" dace is a fun loving fish, who feeds steadily through summer, autumn and winter.

Groundbait effective? YES – see Chapter 12.

Best fishing methods for BIG Dace: Float fishing (see Chapter 14), legering (see Chapter 15) and fly fishing (see Chapter 18).

Right line strength for big dace: At least 0.90 Kg (2 lbs) breaking strain.

EEL

Name: Eel (Anguilla anguilla).
Family: Anguillidae (also called "Apodes"). There are over 500 related species of eel worldwide, including the conger eel and moray eel.
Record rod-caught weight: 5 Kg 46 g (11 lbs 2 oz).
Place caught: Kingfisher Lake, Ringwood, Hampshire (1978).
Caught by: Steve Terry.
Size we can expect to catch: Average weight about 680 g (1½ lbs).
Where eels like to live: All waters; in holes and hollows at the bottom of rivers; deep pools in streams, and particularly lakes, lochs, reservoirs, gravel pits and snag-ridden ponds.

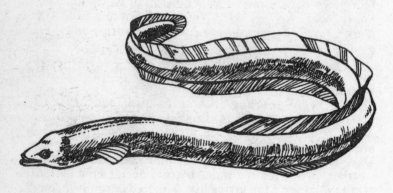

10. Eel.

How to recognise eels: Dark brown or black with silver belly; snake-like appearance.
Sport "Star" rating: ***** Very good fighting fish *****
Eel's favourite natural food: Small fish, frogs, insects, worms, shellfish etc.
Baits to catch eels: Earthworms, cheese paste, chunks of dead herring, sprat or mackerel.
Eel's peak sporting fitness: JUNE/JULY/AUGUST/SEPTEMBER/OCTOBER.
Know your eel: Eel is a mysterious fish. Much about his life

is unknown. Freshwater eels are born in the Sargasso Sea, a vast mass of floating vegetation in the North Atlantic Ocean. Young eels drift in ocean currents for 3 years before entering European rivers and streams as "elvers" (tiny bootlace size eels). Some eels travel overland on damp nights to isolated ponds and remote land-locked waters (eels can live for long periods out of water); slithering adult eels have been seen climbing 1.8 m (6 ft) high obstacles in their quest to find a new watery home. After reaching maturity, most eels return to the Sargasso Sea to breed; then die. Eels don't breed in freshwater. Some adult eels seem to prefer not to make the arduous journey back to the Sargasso Sea; stay put in their freshwater homes and grow huge. Eels of 9 Kg (20 lbs) and above almost certainly exist, but have never been success-fully landed on rod and line.

Eels have a highly developed sense of smell; feed mainly after dusk, especially at night and often track food for considerable distances.

Groundbait effective? YES – see Chapter 12 (include plenty of chopped worms or fish and a little grated cheese).

Best fishing methods for BIG Eels: Legering (see Chapter 15).

Right line strength for big eels: At least 4.53 Kg (10 lbs) breaking strain. Big eels have powerful jaws and small sharp teeth, which may sever line. Many anglers fish for big eels with special fishing *trace wire* attaching hook to line.

GRAYLING

Name: Grayling (Thymallus thymallus).
Family: Salmonidae. Other members of family found in Europe, Asia and northern North America.
Record rod-caught weight: 1 Kg 899 g (4 lbs 3 oz).
Place caught: River Frome, Dorset (1989).
Caught by: S. R. Lanigan.
Size we can expect to catch: Average weight about 340 g (12 oz).
Where grayling like to live: Sparkling-clear, fast flowing rivers and streams. Found in Scotland, northern England; the Midlands and southwest England, especially the chalk streams of Hampshire and Berkshire.

11. Grayling.

How to recognise grayling: Attractive and elegant fish; silver, purple/blue colours flash brightly from its scales. Large eyes and small mouth.

Sport "Star" rating: ****** Excellent fighting fish ******

Grayling's favourite natural food: Flies, insects, snails, worms and water plants.

Baits to catch grayling: Flies (real or artificial), worms, maggots, bread flake etc.

Grayling's peak sporting fitness: JUNE/JULY/AUGUST/ SEPTEMBER/OCTOBER/NOVEMBER/DECEMBER/JANUARY/ FEBRUARY.

Know your grayling: Related to the salmon and trout but officially classed as a "coarse" fish, graceful grayling is known as "Lady of the Stream". Grayling swim in small shoals; feed mostly near the water bottom and mid-water depth, but frequently rise to take flies and insects from the surface.

The shoals rove between holes and hollows at the edge of fast flowing water or streamy runs, and dense growths of weed in deep water.

Grayling feed enthusiastically throughout the year, and when hooked fight with sustained power and tenacity.

Groundbait effective? YES (very small amounts, mainly "feeding") – see Chapter 12.

Best fishing methods for BIG Grayling: Fly fishing (see Chapter 18), float fishing (see Chapter 14) and legering (see Chapter 15).

Right line strength for big grayling: At least 0.90 Kg (2 lbs) breaking strain.

PERCH

Name: Perch (Perca fluviatilis).
Family: Percidae. Other members of family found in Europe, Asia and North America.
Record rod-caught weight: 2 Kg 523 g (5 lbs 9 oz).
Place caught: Private lake, Kent (1985).
Caught by: J. Shayler.
Size we can expect to catch: Average weight about 227 g (8 oz).
Where perch like to live: Quiet ponds, lakes, lochs, canals, gravel pits, rivers and streams across U.K.

12. Perch.

How to recognise perch: Handsome fish. Olive-green back shading into golden-brown, with 5-7 dark green stripes down each side. Spiky top fin; lower fins bright red or orange.
Sport "Star" rating: **** Good fighting fish ****
Perch's favourite natural food: Small fish, worms, shellfish, insects etc.
Baits to catch perch: Worms, maggots, "casters" (see page

48); small chunks of dead sprat or herring.

Perch's peak sporting fitness: JULY/AUGUST/SEPTEMBER/ OCTOBER/NOVEMBER/DECEMBER/JANUARY/FEBRUARY.

Know your perch: Perch's distinctive colouring has earned him names like, "sergeant fish" and "freshwater tiger".

The perch is a predator – hunting and feeding on living or recently dead creatures. Small perch swim in shoals, adolescent perch hunt in packs and large adults live and feed alone; specializing in ambush techniques from hides in weed beds, reeds and thick growths of underwater vegetation.

Perch hunt principally by sight and are attracted by movement. During the summer, they pursue shoals of fish fry in shallows and weeded bankside runs, fully prepared to track their prey over long distances. In winter, perch follow shoals of small fish into deep water and take position in holes and hollows at the water bottom. Perch get peckish all year, especially in winter, when surviving young fish are wiser and more difficult for perch to catch.

Groundbait effective? YES (very small amounts, mainly "cloud" to draw fish fry, which attract perch) - see Chapter 12.

Best fishing methods for BIG Perch: Legering (see Chapter 15), spinning (see Chapter 19) and float fishing (see Chapter 14).

Right line strength for big perch: At least 1.36 Kg (3 lbs) breaking strain.

PIKE

Name: Pike (Esox lucius).

Family: Esocidae. Other members of family found in Europe, northern Asia and North America.

Record rod-caught weight: 21 Kg 234 g (46 lbs 13 oz).

Place caught: Llandergfedd, Wales (1992).

Caught by: R. Lewis.

Size we can expect to catch: Average weight about 3.62 Kg (8 lbs).

Where pike like to live: Flowing and still waters throughout Britain; lakes, lochs, ponds, gravel pits, reservoirs, rivers and streams. Among the best known haunts of monster pike are the Norfolk Broads, Hampshire Avon and Loch Lomond.

13. Pike.

How to recognise pike: Distinctive green and yellow camouflage markings, varying in shade and pattern from one water to another. Long body, forked tail; strong jaws and shark-like teeth!

Sport "Star" rating: ***** Very good fighting fish *****

Pike's favourite natural food: Fish, frogs, frog spawn, water birds, rats, voles, worms, insects.

Baits to catch pike: Dead herring, sprat or mackerel; earthworms.

Pike's peak sporting fitness: JULY/AUGUST/SEPTEMBER/OCTOBER/NOVEMBER/DECEMBER/JANUARY.

Know your pike: Pike is an immensely powerful, awe-inspiring fish. His nickname – "freshwater shark", describes the terror with which monster pike have always been regarded. Pike's mouth is equipped with hundreds of sharp, inward pointing teeth – once they snap shut on a victim, there's no escape!

Few baits are too large for big pike to swallow. Ducks are frequent prey and swans have been reported attacked. A pike of 32.65 Kg (72 lbs) was caught on Loch Ken in 1774; an old and dying pike of 27.21 Kg (60 lbs) was found at Dowdeswell.

Pike lurk at the water bottom behind screening stones; in holes, hollows and bank undercuts, and hide in weed, reed and lily beds. They hunt mostly by eyesight; feed mainly in daylight and make their kills by speedy acceleration to bushwhack unsuspecting fish.

Although pike prefer eating flesh, they do seize insects and in summertime sometimes bask near the surface; soaking up sun.

Pike feed in patterns − definite times and locations that alter after a period of days or weeks, seemingly related to weather, wind and temperature changes. In summer, pike often feed alone and at dawn; occasionally hunting in packs, making planned attacks on shoals of fish. Solitary hunting and pack attacks continue in winter. Mid-day can be a productive time to fish for pike on cold days.

Pike feed wherever fish congregate, and are caught in still or slow moving, deep water; also near shallows and fast flowing bankside runs.

Even small streams may hold pike of 3.62 Kg (8 lbs) in weight.

Groundbait effective? YES (small amounts of chopped fish and/or worms) - see Chapter 12.

Best fishing methods for BIG Pike: Legering (see Chapter 15) and spinning (see Chapter 19).

Right line strength for big pike: At least 5.44 Kg (12 lbs) breaking strain. Because pike have sharp teeth that can easily cut through line, it's wise to fish with special fishing *trace wire* attaching hook to line.

NOTE: Remove hooks from pike with an angler's hook disgorger, forceps or pliers. To hold open big pike's jaws safely while removing your hook, gently fix an angler's *pike gag.*

ROACH

Name: Roach (Rutilus rutilus).
Family: Cyprinidae. Other members of family found in Europe, Africa and Asia.
Record rod-caught weight: 1 Kg 899 g (4 lbs 3 oz).
Place caught: River Stour, Dorset (1990).

Caught by: Ramon Clarke.
Size we can expect to catch: Average size about 170 g (6 oz).
Where roach like to live: Slow flowing rivers; canals, lakes, pits, ponds and reservoirs in most parts of Britain, except northern Scotland.

Dolphins Barn Branch Tel. 4540681

14. Roach.

How to recognise roach: Dark green or blue-brown back; silvery sides and belly. Red eyes and reddish fins; small mouth with projecting upper lip.
Sport "Star" rating: ***** Very good fighting fish *****
Roach's favourite natural food: Vegetable matter, insects etc.
Baits to catch roach: Sweetcorn, hempseed, pearl barley, tares, bread flake or paste, maggots, "casters" (see page 48), cheese paste, worms, caddis grubs and silkweed.
Roach's peak sporting fitness: JULY/AUGUST/SEPTEMBER/ OCTOBER/NOVEMBER/DECEMBER/JANUARY/FEBRUARY.
Know your roach: Roach is a sociable shoal fish. He has a healthy appetite and feeds contentedly in warm and cold weather. Smaller shoal roach sun themselves in shallow water in summer, ducking in and out of weed and lily roots. Large roach don't seem to like bright light and stay deep in hot weather, feeding in the cool of early morning or late evening.

Roach shoals patrol a regular beat; inspecting water plants, whirling eddies and edges of fast runs for food. But they hide out of sight; alter patrol times and occasionally vacate an area in moments, only to return a short while later.

Roach are basically bottom- or near bottom-feeding fish, although in summer they rise to seize insects on the water surface. During winter roach remain at the bottom of deep water.

Groundbait effective? YES – see Chapter 12.

Best fishing methods for BIG Roach: Float fishing (see Chapter 14) and legering (see Chapter 15).

Right line strength for big roach: At least 1.36 Kg (3 lbs) breaking strain.

RUDD

Name: Rudd (Scardinius erythrophthalmus).

Family: Cyprinidae. Other members of family found in Europe, Africa and Asia.

Record rod-caught weight: 2 Kg 97 g (4 lbs 10 oz).

Place caught: Pitsford Reservoir, Northants. (1986).

Caught by: D. Webb.

Size we can expect to catch: Average weight about 141 g (5 oz).

Where rudd like to live: Widespread in England, Wales and Ireland. Found in lakes, ponds, gravel pits and quiet stretches of rivers.

15. Rudd.

How to recognise rudd: Beautiful fish, golden/yellow colour; yellow-orange eyes, reddish lips and rich red fins.
Sport "Star" rating: **** Good fighting fish ****
Rudd's favourite natural food: Insects, water plants, worms and shellfish.
Baits to catch rudd: Worms, maggots, bread flake, cheese paste, caddis grubs etc.
Rudd's peak sporting fitness: JULY/AUGUST/SEPTEMBER/OCTOBER/NOVEMBER.
Know your rudd: Rudd is a summer surface-feeding shoal fish. He stays close to water plants, weed beds, reeds and lily pads. Shoals also make for bankside runs of water beneath overhanging bushes and trees to snap falling insects.

The shoal's surface sucking sounds are clearly audible on quiet summer's days.

Rudd reduce feeding in winter months and can be tricky to catch; they stay near the water bottom; take limited amounts of food at irregular intervals - livening up at noon on sunny-warm winter's days.

Big rudd occasionally snatch scraps of food from the water bottom, summer and winter.
Groundbait effective? YES - see Chapter 12.
Best fishing methods for BIG Rudd: Float fishing (see Chapter 14), fly fishing (see Chapter 18) and legering (see Chapter 15).
Right line strength for big rudd: At least 0.90 Kg (2 lbs) breaking strain.

TENCH

Name: Tench (Tinca tinca).
Family: Cyprinidae. Other members of family found in Europe, Africa and Asia.
Record rod-caught weight: 6 Kg 548 g (14 lbs 7 oz).
Place caught: Private gravel pit, Hertfordshire (1993).
Caught by: G. Beaven.
Size we can expect to catch: Average weight about 1.36 Kg (3 lbs).
Where tench like to live: On the bottom of heavily weeded lakes, ponds, canals, and slow flowing waters. Widely distributed throughout U.K.

16. Tench.

How to recognise tench: Smooth, dark olive/golden scales; small barbule (feeler) at each side of the upper lip. Large rounded fins and small red eyes.

Sport "Star" rating: **** Good fighting fish ****

Tench's favourite natural food: Insects, shellfish, worms and vegetable matter.

Baits to catch tench: Bread flake, bread paste, maggots, sweetcorn, worms.

Tench's peak sporting fitness: JUNE/JULY/AUGUST/ SEPTEMBER/OCTOBER.

Know your tench: Tench is a handsome, shy shoal fish. Tench wander along the bottom of quiet, weedy and reedy waters in small groups; shovelling, grubbing and feeling for scraps of food with their barbules (feelers) and fins. Patches of bubbles bursting on the water surface may betray their presence. Tench feed enthusiastically only in warm, bright summer months; early morning and evening are the best times to catch tench. Summer early morning anglers see tench rolling lazily on the surface. Big tench frequently feed near the bank and sometimes investigate areas of the water bottom deliberately stirred or raked by tench anglers to release particles of appetizing natural food.

Although normally passive fish, tench are strong fighters when hooked.

A tench of 5 Kg (11 lbs) was hooked and landed from a pit at Wraysbury, Middlesex in July, 1959 – but put back before being examined and accepted as a record breaker.
Groundbait effective? YES - see Chapter 12.
Best fishing methods for BIG Tench: Legering (see Chapter 15) and float fishing (see Chapter 14).
Right line strength for big tench: At least 2.26 Kg (5 lbs) breaking strain.

TROUT

Name: Trout, brown (Salmo trutta).
Family: Salmonidae. Other members of family found in Europe, Asia and North America.
Record rod-caught weight: 8 Kg 912 g (19 lbs 10 oz).
Place caught: Loch Awe, Scotland (1993).
Caught by: A. Thorne.
Size we can expect to catch: Average weight about 0.90 Kg (2 lbs).
Where trout like to live: Lakes, lochs, pits, reservoirs, rivers and streams. All waters that are clear, clean and well oxygenated.

17. Trout.

How to recognise trout: The "brown" trout can be various colours spanning yellow/brown with brightly coloured spots and rings, to silver, speckled with black spots.

Sport "Star" rating: ****** Excellent fighting fish ******

Trout's favourite natural food: Flies, insects, worms, small fish, shellfish etc.

Baits to catch trout: Flies (real or artificial) and worms.

Trout's peak sporting fitness: MARCH/APRIL/MAY/JUNE/ JULY/AUGUST/SEPTEMBER.

Know your trout: Trout is a great individualist; cunning, adaptable and robust, he lives and hunts alone; guarding his own water territory with courage and ferocity.

Rainbow trout (introduced to Europe from North America) are stocked with brown trout in many stillwaters. American brook trout are also stocked in some stillwaters. Sea trout (silvery in colour) are brown trout that have chosen to live in the sea; returning to rivers and streams to spawn.

All trout may be fished for successfully using similar tackle and methods.

Adult brown trout living in a narrow stream might be small, but trout can grow huge, depending upon size and depth of water and food supply.

Scotland is the home of monster brown trout and fish approaching 9 Kg (20 lbs) are caught on some of the larger lochs. In 1866, W. Muir took 2½ hours to land a foul hooked (accidentally hooked – see page 116) brown trout from Loch Awe. The fish weighed 17.91 Kg (39 lbs 8 oz)! The body was preserved and displayed in a case, but unfortunately this historic trophy was later destroyed by fire.

Good sport may be had fly fishing for trout. However, big trout are often exclusively cannibal; eating only smaller fish and seldom, if ever, rise from deep water to take insects at the surface.

Hooked trout are wild and fierce fighters; jumping, somersaulting and diving to dislodge your hook or smash the line. Even after being landed the fighting gymnastics continue.

Groundbait effective? NO.

Best fishing methods for BIG Trout: Spinning (see Chapter 19) and fly fishing (see Chapter 18). Refer also to "Top twenty trout tips", starting on page 109.

Right line strength for big trout: At least 2.26 Kg (5 lbs) breaking strain.

ZANDER

Name: Zander, also known as Pikeperch (Stizostedion lucioperca).
Family: Percidae. Other members of family found in Europe and North America.
Record rod-caught weight: 8 Kg 391 g (18 lbs 8 oz).
Place caught: Cambridge stillwater (1988).
Caught by: R. N. Meadows.
Size we can expect to catch: Average weight about 1.81 Kg (4 lbs).
Where zander like to live: Lakes and rivers. Common in Europe, introduced to U.K. in 1878 at Woburn Abbey Lake. In 1963, 97 tiny zander were released into the Great Ouse Relief Channel. They bred and spread fast. Mainly found in East Anglia, also stocked in some Club waters.

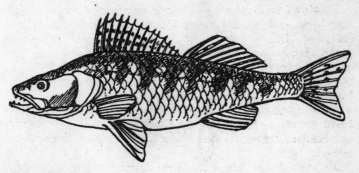

18. Zander.

How to recognise zander: Long, perch-like body. Greenish-grey back and silvery belly. Large mouth and sharp teeth!
Sport "Star" rating: **** Good fighting fish ****
Zander's favourite natural food: Small fish, worms, insects.
Baits to catch zander: Chunks of dead herring, sprat or

mackerel, worms, maggots.

Zander's peak sporting fitness: JULY/AUGUST/SEPTEMBER/ OCTOBER/NOVEMBER/DECEMBER/JANUARY/FEBRUARY.

Know your zander: Zander is cousin to the perch. He feeds deep down in water; hunting in packs that tear into shoals of small fish; often biting, ripping and spitting out its prey several times before swallowing the bits. Sometimes, in cat-and-mouse fashion, zander "plays" with its victim until, having made the kill, zander loses interest and leaving the dead victim, moves on.

Zander can scent and track food across considerable distances; feeding happily in muddy and murky water.

Groundbait effective? YES – see Chapter 12 (include plenty of chopped worms or fish).

Best fishing methods for BIG Zander: Legering (see Chapter 15) and spinning (see Chapter 19).

Right line strength for big zander: At least 3.62 Kg (8 lbs) breaking strain. Big zander have sharp teeth, which can cut through line. Some anglers prefer to fish for big zander with special fishing *trace wire* attaching hook to line.

NOTE: Remove hooks from big zander with an angler's hook disgorger, forceps, or pliers.

6

WRAP UP AND KIT OUT

Fun fishing for sport can be foul and fretful when we are not comfy and cosy.

Wrap up right, kit out correctly and be merry come rain or snow. Jack Frost's ice fingers won't freeze our fishing fun.

Weather fools us every time we go fishing. Don't be caught out. Be prepared and stay smiling.

Get sacked
Rucksacks, daysacs or pacsacs strap over your shoulders; hold all the gear and leave your arms free.

Get a sac of some sort. You come to love your sac as it shares fishing adventures and provides food, drink, tackle, waterproofs and warming woollens in moments of need.

Wrap up
Socks
In winter wear two pairs of socks. Wool socks are warmest; let your feet breathe and reduce sweating. Two pairs keep your feet super snug and stop bruising if you have to walk a distance over rough ground.

Long pants or tights
Thermal, ankle-length pants, pyjama trousers or tights worn underneath trousers give extra insulation in cold weather. Ladies are happy wearing tights, but I know a man who wears his wife's tights winter fishing. We call him Patsy. He doesn't seem to mind and is warm as toast in the coldest weather.

Trousers
Jeans are not good. An old pair of trousers is best. Denim jeans and cords offer little warmth.

Vest, shirt and pullovers

A thermal vest is valued in winter. Wear a shirt and one or two pullovers. Two light pullovers give more warmth than one heavy pullover. Even in summer have at least one pullover handy; chill air often creeps across your chest at the water's edge to cause discomfort.

Hats and things

A woolly hat that pulls over your ears keeps the brains warm. Much of our body heat is lost through the head, and a woollen scarf wrapped round your neck stops icy rain trickling down your back.

Handy *fingerless* woollen or thermal *fishing mitts* are helpful, and a stout pair of *leather walking boots* a welcome investment.

Sudden rain is not unknown in the U.K. and a set of inexpensive *waterproofs* folded into your rucksack saves a wearisome wetting.

Home comforts

We don't have to leave all comforts at home. Pack sandwiches, a flask of warm soup and a couple of chocolate bars. Have a nibble when the fish aren't biting. Don't forget insect repellant in the summer, or you'll be on the menu!

7

TACKLE

Good tackle helps catch big fish. Lots of tackle is on sale to today's angler, but the key to success is *your* ability to use tackle correctly and with confidence when hooking and landing fighting fish.

Buy best
Buy the best quality tackle you can afford. Buying cheap costs dear in the long run.

Quality tackle is produced by experts. You pay extra for their know-how and guarantee of excellence. Makers of quality tackle provide an after-sales maintenance and repair service. Their address is included in catalogues and with products.

Cheap tackle frequently doesn't work well, breaks; loses large fish and requires constant repair, or replacing.

Know your dealer
Get to know your local specialist tackle dealer. Visit his shop and view the huge amounts of tackle on display. Leaf through some catalogues; see the fishing newspapers, magazines and books offered for sale.

All tackle dealers are friendly and helpful fishing experts. Chat to your dealer; ask his advice about tackle, baits, local fishing clubs and contests.

Your tackle dealer is wise, buy all you need for fishing from him and have no worries.

Rods
Special rods are designed for:
Float fishing (see Chapter 14) to cast light lines long distances and give maximum float and line control; *legering* (see Chapter 15); to cast heavy weights and baits, and *spinning* (see Chapter 19) to cast and rapidly retrieve strong lines and weighty artificial lures. *Pole fishing* (see Chapter

16) and *fly fishing* (see Chapter 18) also need specialized rods. However most types of fishing may be enjoyed successfully with a general purpose rod of 3 m (10 feet) to 3.65 m (12 feet) in length.

Selection of specialist rods is best discussed with your local tackle dealer, who'll let you try rods in his shop before you buy.

Reels

Reliable reels are vital to fishing success. Buy the best you can afford. Describe to your tackle dealer the sort of fishing you intend doing. He'll guide your choice. A reel suitable for general purpose fishing is unlike one made for competition match anglers; reels for heavy pike spinning, or gentle fly fishing are highly individual in design and performance.

For effective casting always fill your reel fully with line.

Line

Your line connects you to the hooked fish. Poor quality line is the fishes' friend. Don't be parted from your catch – buy good line!

Competition match anglers often fish fine lines of about 0.5 Kg (1 lb) breaking strain; some specimen hunters, chasing big fish, use lines of 2.26 Kg (5 lbs) to 4.5 Kg (10 lbs) breaking strain and sometimes stronger, depending on the species they're after (see suggested line strength for big fish in each fish's "Fish file", Chapter 5).

A good general purpose line should have a breaking strain of at least 1.36 Kg (3 lbs).

Floats

There's a float for every fishing situation (see Chapter 14). Most of us collect too many floats and rarely use half of them! Buy a few carefully chosen floats and from experience find how to fish them correctly before adding more floats to your collection.

Landing net

A length-adjustable (telescopic) landing net is a must. The longer the handle when fully extended and larger the net, the better. Never let a surprise huge fish escape because you can't get your fish out of the water before it smashes the line.

Hooks

Your choice of hook size depends on the bait you wish to fish (see Chapter 8). Hooks without a barb (sharp inward projecting piece of wire at hook point) penetrate better and are easier and quicker to free from the fish's mouth; this may prove vital in competition match fishing (see Chapter 17). However, barbed hooks are better for wriggly baits like maggots or worms, which don't always want to stay on barbless hooks.

Odds and bits

All sorts of optional extras are on sale in your local tackle shop including: angler's thermal and waterproof clothing, bait and bait containers, bait aprons for match anglers, battery headlamps for night fishing, catapults for long distance ground-baiting, electronic bite alarms, eye shades, float caps, polarised sun glasses, reel pouches, rod bags, rod rests, scissors, swivels, tackle boxes, umbrellas, vacuum flasks, and weights.

Sound advice

Discuss tackle purchases with your specialist tackle dealer and *listen* to his sound advice. Aim to use the least amount of tackle necessary to catch fish; choose recommended tackle *you* like the feel and look of; buy the best you can afford, and remember that although good quality tackle helps catch big fish, there is no substitute for your intelligence, cunning and hunting skill.

D.I.Y.

Fancy making your own value-for-money "customized" tackle – rods, floats, fly-tying etc? Instruction books and tackle making kits are stocked by your dealer, or can be ordered for you.

Security

Watch out – there are thieves about!
   Record serial numbers marked on your equipment: etch tackle with your own easily identifiable secret symbol; insure tackle against theft and damage. Glue or sew an address label to rucksacks, tackle bags or boxes. Don't forget to give your telephone number. Sometimes stolen or mislaid tackle turns up in the most unlikely places!

8

BAITS AND BREEDING

Many baits can be bought from tackle dealers; some are ordinary foods available from food stores – a few baits you may choose to breed.

Baits similar to the natural foods found in the water you plan fishing are likely to be highly effective when fished with skill; easily fooling fish into accepting your bait as safely familiar, tasty food.

Finding bait the natural way
For an exciting and challenging way to fish, search the waterside for the fishes' normal food immediately before you begin fishing. Then you know your natural bait is fresh and eagerly sought by the fish.

Where to look
Under piles of rotting leaves, weed or rushes; fallen branches and rotten tree stumps for worms, woodlice, earwigs, grubs and beetles. Check chewed fresh leaves for caterpillars and watch for ripe berries growing near the water.

Wrigglies' Liberation Front
If you believe worms, maggots and other wrigglies need love and understanding and you are loth to spike them on a hook and drown them; stick to bread, cheese, fruit, grain, meat, vegetables, artificial spinning lures and artificial flies – these all attract big fish too!

Push the point
To make sure that fish taking your bait bite the hook point; push your hook through whatever bait you are using until the sharp hook point protrudes. Then the bait won't stop your hook penetrating the fish's lip when the line is tightened.

Get fresh
For best results leave buying or gathering and preparing your baits until the last convenient moment before fishing.
The fresher your bait; the finer your catch!

Hook sizes: A word in your ear.
Choose a hook size to suit your bait. Suggested hook sizes are given for most baits detailed on the following pages of this Chapter. However, these hook sizes are *suggestions* only. The bigger your bait, the bigger the hook and vice-versa.

Bread
Use your loaf to hook fish.

Crust
Suggested hook sizes: 12 or 14 or 16
At the waterside; rinse your hands, then pluck a hunk of crust from the top of freshly baked, unsliced white bread. Some fluffy white bread attached to the crust is desirable.

Cubes
Suggested hook sizes: 8 or 10 or 12 or 14
At home, cut a 6 mm (¼ inch) thick crust from the end of a freshly baked unsliced white loaf; lay the crust on a large *clean* cloth; cover crust with the cloth; place on a hard, flat surface and leave to press under a heavy weight (wooden board, heavy saucepan etc.) for 2 hours. Then cut into cubes.

Flake
Suggested hook sizes: 10 or 12 or 14
At the waterside, use the fluffy bread flake plucked from the *inside* of an unsliced freshly baked white loaf.

Paste
Suggested hook sizes: 8 or 10 or 12
At the waterside, rinse your hands; then – in a suitable bowl – mix some of the water with a little stale white bread several days' old. Don't make too much at once. Knead until soft and tacky – a texture judged to be right for staying on your hook.
    Appetizing extras sometimes add appeal to bread paste and bring spectacular success. Among popular titbits that

can be popped into your paste mix are: bananas (ripe), cheese (grated), cheese (spready), chocolate powder (drinking), custard powder, fruit (soft), honey, meat pastes, soup powder, and yeast extract spreads.

Pellets
Suggested hook sizes: 14 or 16 or 18
At the waterside, use a bread punch (available from your tackle dealer) to punch pellets from a freshly baked white loaf.

Maggots
Suggested hook sizes: three maggots on size 10 or 12; two maggots on size 14; one maggot on size 16
Maggots are larvae hatched from flies' eggs. They're bred commercially on maggot farms and sold by many specialist tackle dealers. A maggot develops into a chrysalis (or "case") known to anglers as a *caster* before emerging as a fly.

Maggots and casters are valuable fish catching baits. To slow down your lively maggots' change into unmoving "casters", keep them somewhere shaded and cool before and during fishing.

Sympathetic womenfolk sometimes let us store fresh, securely bait-boxed, maggots for a day or three in the family fridge.

A water-tight container may be stood in a covered bowl, bucket or watering can partly filled with cold water and hidden in a shady spot.

The warmer your maggots are, the sooner they'll turn into casters.

Summer maggot breeding
To breed your own maggots when summer comes, buy a small piece of cheap meat (heart is ideal). Slash three deep cuts in the meat; then put the meat in a suitable container – bucket; box etc. Place container outside after dark; we're after the big, juicy maggots that hatch from eggs laid by the night-flying *callyphora erythrocephalia*. Fit a lid or covering allowing a small space for an adult fly to enter.

Watch out for marauding cats! Put the container somewhere safe.

Next morning look for white patches of flies' eggs. Each patch of eggs is called a "blow" and will produce *dozens* of maggots. Fasten an airtight lid during the daytime. Repeat the procedure for one or two more nights. Several "blows" supply sufficient maggots to last a few lengthy fishing trips.

If your meat is blessed with too many "blows", you can scrape off unwanted eggs with a knife.

Wrap the "blown" meat in a couple of sheets of clean newspaper. Pour *bran* over the paper-wrapped blown meat to form a layer about 25 mm (1 inch) deep over the container base. Fasten a lid with *tiny* pricked or bored holes; alternatively, secure over the container top with string or elastic, a piece of cloth or nylon (stretched old tights, curtain etc.) or pin-pricked plastic sheeting.

Keep somewhere cool and dark for 7 days; then transfer hatched maggots into your bait box. Throw away decomposing meat and smelly bran. Add some fresh bran to your bait box to warm and nourish the maggots. Then store in cool. Your maggots are ready for use.

*** TIP ***
Always keep your "live" bait alive and wriggling by storing it in a bait container with tiny air holes pricked in the lid.

*** TIP ***
When hooking live "wriggling" bait, simply nick your hook point through the skin; leaving the bait maximum freedom of "natural" movement in the water. Deep hooking quickly kills your bait, which is then less tempting to fish.

Worms
Bloodworms
Suggested hook sizes: 18 or 22
Larvae ("grub" stage) of the midge fly. Found in mud at the water bottom. Best bought from your specialist tackle dealer.

Brandlings
Suggested hook sizes: 18 or 22
Red and yellow banded worm. Found in compost heaps, manure and among rotting leaves. Easily bred in home-made "wormery" – an old sink, aquarium etc. with a 25 mm (1 inch) deep pebble base for drainage; covered with leaves and alternate layers of soil and old potato peelings, tea leaves, apple cores etc. Keep covered in a cool, dry place.

Regularly water soil to dampness with collected rain water and feed worms with tiny scraps of leftover vegetable and fruit. Remove any diseased or dead brandlings you come across.

Earthworms (lobworms)
Suggested hook sizes: 6 or 8 or 10
Found under large stones and in shaded, damp soil. Encourage earthworms to a specific area of your garden by daily emptying tea leaves from the teapot or split tea bags. Keep soil rich and damp and you'll always be able to fork up a few worms for fishing.

Earthworms can also be collected above ground on close cut grass after rain, or at night. Tread quietly; after dark use a torch with beam dimmed by handkerchief or tissue.

For ace results aim to store earthworms for a couple or more days in damp moss before fishing – a week is ideal. Moss makes worms lively, tough skinned (for staying on your hook) and doubly appealing to fish!

Remove any dead or sickly worms.

19.   The right way to hook a worm.

Taking worms fishing
When you take worms fishing, keep them in a bait container filled with moss or damp newspaper (not soil) and *never* mix worms with maggots. Why? Because maggots *eat* worms. Use separate containers.

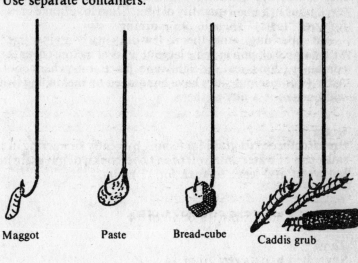

Maggot   Paste   Bread-cube   Caddis grub

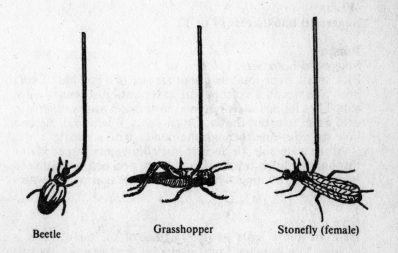

Beetle   Grasshopper   Stonefly (female)

20.   A selection of hooked baits.

Slugs
Suggested hook sizes: 6 or 8
Gather slugs from their dark, damp hideouts, or sink slug traps (empty, unwanted plastic cartons/food containers) into soil before nightfall, with the open mouth at ground level; pour in a *small* quantity of beer. Slugs love home brew! Remove "merry" slugs in the morning.

For super slugs, store them a few days in a container lined with damp soil; pop in some large chunks of melon, cover the container (don't seal air-tight) and place somewhere cool. After your luscious slugs have banqueted on melon, big fish will queue for a bite at them.

Grain
Prepare uncooked grain for fishing by gently simmering in a saucepan of water until soft (don't overcook); or put grain in hot water and leave to soak for 12 hours.

Hempseed
Suggested hook sizes: 18 or 16 or 14

Tares
Suggested hook sizes: 16 or 14

Wheat
Suggested hook sizes: 14 or 12

Potato
Suggested hook size: 1/0 or 1 or 2
Pick small, firm potatoes about the size of a golf ball. Don't peel. Simmer in a saucepan of water until just tender – not soft. Then immediately remove the potatoes and submerse in cold water to arrest the cooking process. When cold, pierce a hole for your line through the potato with a needle.

At the waterside, tie hook to line *after* you've threaded line through the hole. Break off a piece of peel before casting to reveal some inviting white potato flesh against the water bottom.

Give it a go!
Here are more baits to try. The list of successful baits is endless. New ones are found every day. Fish seem to like soft baits better than hard baits, but apart from this preference

anything goes – experiment, experiment, experiment!

Where appropriate, suggested hook sizes are bracketed next to baits; choose a hook size to suit the size of bait you're fishing.

*** TIP ***
A combination of two different baits on one hook often draws special attention from greedy fish.

All-sorts
Bacon – fatty / baked bean (14 or 16) / banana chunk – ripe / beetroot – diced / berries – general (12 or 14 or 16) / blackberry (8) / blackcurrant (14) / bluebottle / caddis grub – in or out of its case / carrot – diced and lightly boiled / cheese – ripe and smelly / cherry – stone removed (12) / chocolate – soft centre (6) / currant (14 or 16) / herring – dead – hooked through eye sockets (2) / luncheon meat – chopped into chunks / macaroni – boiled – with a little grated cheese worked in as an appetizer / mussels – freshwater – removed from shell (8 or 6) / peas (14 or 16) / sausage – whole or part – lightly boiled (2 or 4 or 6) / silkweed – wrapped around hook (10 or 12 or 14) / spaghetti – boiled / sprat – dead – hooked through eye sockets (2) / sultana (14 or 16) / sweetcorn – two grains (10) / tomato – sliced / etc., etc.

9

KNOW KNOT SENSE

We must know and practise our knots. Big fish strain our line, and the weakest point in line is usually a wrongly tied or unsuitable knot. When we lose rod-bending fish through line parting from hooks or knotted joins, we have ourselves to blame. So know knot sense and get knotted right.

Knots are great fun to learn and always useful to know – once knotted, never forgotted!

Reel knot

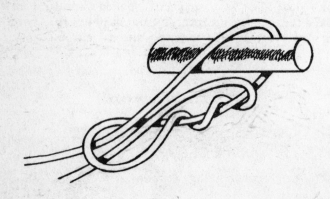

21. Reel knot.

For attaching line to reel.

Tucked half blood knot

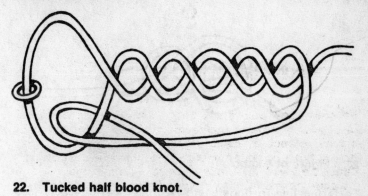

22. Tucked half blood knot.

For tying eyed hooks, artificial flies, lures or swivels to line.

Loop knot

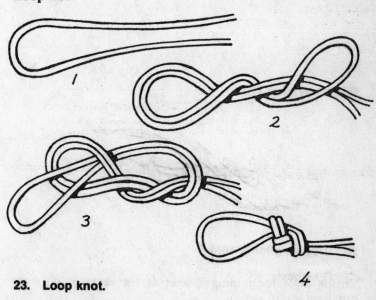

23. Loop knot.

To make a loop for securing hooklength (see page 64) or leader (see page 100) to line.

Figure of 8 knot

24. Figure of 8 knot.

To fasten line to hooklength (see page 64) or leader (see page 100).

Double grinner knot

25. Double grinner knot.

Strong knot for joining 2 lines of the same or different breaking strain.

Stop knot

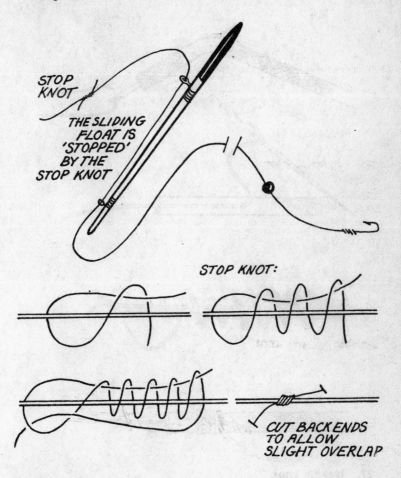

STOP KNOT

STOP KNOT

THE SLIDING FLOAT IS 'STOPPED' BY THE STOP KNOT

STOP KNOT:

CUT BACK ENDS TO ALLOW SLIGHT OVERLAP

26.   Stop knot.

For stopping a "sliding float" at pre-set depth when fishing deep water (see page 84).

Needle knot

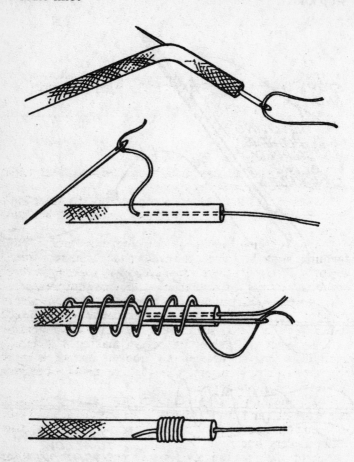

27. Needle knot.

To tie fly line to backing line (see page 100).

10

MAKE MANNERS MATTER

At the waterside
We must consider our fellow fishers.

"Manners maketh man" and thoughtful behaviour by the waterside makes us better sports.

Let's approach our chosen fishing site quietly; biting back the temptation to shout, "Any luck, mate?" at bankside anglers.

Avoid rubbing shoulders with someone fishing your favourite spot. Too close, and tangled tackle leads to frayed tempers. Hopefully there's room for us all – allow plenty of space and others will appreciate your thoughtfulness.

Ignore huge fish pulling faces from the stretch of water in front of your neighbour. Don't cast across your neighbour's patch. We shall settle scores with that fish sometime soon.

Look over your shoulder before making a sweeping overhead cast. An accidentally hooked human is more frightening than the biggest pike – believe me! Hooked trees are also cruel opponents.

Loud sploshing and splashing of cast line or groundbait can scare fish and anger fishermen. Be quiet to stay friends.

Keep your hooked fish under tight control and away from other anglers' lines.

Accept the fact we always see monster size fish the moment our tackle is packed ready for the journey home.

Remember there will be another day!

Away from the water
To keep on happy terms with your family, don't practise casting indoors.

Resist temptation to brag about enormous fish caught. Your pals know how good you are. By not making them feel small, you look big.

Ten Commandments

Hear, O fisher for fun and sport, these words. Learn by them and be forever praised for your good deeds. Be a hero among men.

1. Thou shalt NOT fish without permission or the right licence.
2. If thou bicycle, motorcycle or drivest to fish, parkest thine machine thoughtfully; block not others in or out (or thou wilt be sorry!).
3. Neither shalt thou be a "dumbo" and make noise or nuisance of thyself to others.
4. Thou shalt NOT leave gates open; trample flowers, reeds or break down bits of bank.
5. Neither shalt thou deliberately disturb river animals, be they birds, beasties or insects.
6. Nor wilt ye cause cruel pain to fish caught. But having enjoyed the fish's sport return him gently to his watery home.
7. Keep thou away from the edge of banks by deep or fast flowing water, in case thou fallest in – SPLOSH –and get wet or even drowned.
8. Never step ye into fast flowing water of unknown depth. Lest ye be not seen again.
9. Leave not any tackle by the waterside. Especially check thy line, weights and hooks to maketh sure *none* is spread upon the ground.
10. Takest ALL litter home and BIN IT there.

Do these Great Things, O Wise One, and be wiser still!

At all times
Keep calm, think before you act; treat others as you would
like to be treated and make manners matter.

11

SECRETS OF SUCCESS – THINK FISH

Once we understand how fish think, and why they behave as they do, we become more successful at catching them.

Study the "Fish file" (Chapter 5). Each species of fish has developed its own specialized technique for survival, incorporating cunning tricks and dodges.

Starting out
Outsmarting fish starts at home, before you go fishing. Leave brightly coloured clothes and flashy-white shirts in the drawer. Wear drab camouflage colours that blend with bankside vegetation. Pop a pair of polarised sun-glasses in your pocket and pack a peaked cap, or floppy wide-brimmed hat, or angler's eyeshade. Wearing hat or eyeshade and polarised glasses (even in dull weather) reduces water and background glare; hiding fish become visible!

Check you've got all your tackle. Don't forget to take a spare copy of this book and a notebook and pen or pencil (wrapped in a protective plastic bag) for handy waterside reference and important jottings (see Chapter 22).

Timing
Remember, many fish feed ravenously at dawn and dusk (often in the shallows) because at these quiet times the light is changing and fish have the edge over insects and other prey that can't re-focus vision as rapidly as fish can. After feasting, fish take about 12 hours to digest food completely, so may not seek another meal until much later in the day.

Fish are cold-blooded; their body temperature is dependent on the water temperature. The warmer water is, the more active fish become. Busy fish use energy fast and must feed to replenish energy reserves. Therefore, expect fish to feed more frequently in warm weather; less determinedly on cold days. Sudden drops in temperature usually put fish off their food – sometimes for several days!

Reading water

Learn to "read" water. With practice you'll be able to look at any area of water and know whereabouts to fish for particular species. Sketches to help you read waters are included in this Chapter on this page and pages 65 and 66.

28.   Fish haunts in a river:

1, 2 and 3: Roach are usually near weed beds.

4 and 5: Large perch like holes near bank.

6: Mouths of inflowing streams are good for chub.

7: Deep runs near and among weed are favoured by pike.

8: Fast water is liked by dace and grayling.

9: Eddies and runs near bankside rushes may hold chub, roach and dace.

10: Barbel like deep water.

11: Bream and tench prefer slow, sluggish water.

Waterside approach

Put your tackle together away from the waterside. Approach the water quietly; crouch low and move from cover to cover.

Stay well back from the water; don't get close enough to admire your reflection, or cast a telltale shadow across the surface.

Plumbing

To find by "plumbing" the exact depth of the water you're going to fish:

a) Slip a movable float onto your rod line.

b) Tie an angler's *plummet* weight (or suitably heavy weight) to the end of your line.

c) Slide your float up the line to the approximate (guessed) depth of the water and fasten float in position.

d) Accurately cast line and plummet weight – soft entry into water, no splash.

You've gauged the depth when your float is bobbing upright on the water surface. Simply measure the length of line between plummet and float.

Establishing the precise depth of water can be important to all methods of fishing, especially float fishing (see Chapter 14) and spinning (see Chapter 19).

Thermometer

A special angler's thermometer, attached to your line in addition to (or in place of) a plummet weight, increases your knowledge of water conditions; supplies valuable figures for record keeping and may advance our appreciation of fish feeding patterns peculiar to particular species and waters.

Hooklength

Some anglers like to fish with a fine (low breaking strain) "hooklength" line securing hook to main reel line. For right knots, see Chapter 9.

A "hooklength" line should be between 304 mm (12 inches) and 609 mm (24 inches) long, cut from a spool of ordinary fishing line.

The advantages of fishing with a hooklength are:

Hooklength line is less visible to fish than the heavier main reel line.

If a big fish snags and breaks the hooklength line, your float (if any) and/or weights (if any), fixed to the main line, won't be lost.

The disadvantage is that an unexpectedly large hooked

29. A carp lake showing likely fishing spots:
1. During daytime carp like to browse and bask among and near weed beds.
2. Deep water near shaded banks is a favourite place.
3. Near lily pads and bush-shaded banks are also favourites.
4. At night-time carp come close to shore to forage among weeds and rushes.

fish is likely to smash a hooklength line and escape.

Although a hooklength line can be any strength slightly below the main reel line strength, the most popular hooklength line strengths range from 453 g (1 lb) to 1.36 Kg (3 lbs) breaking strain depending on the species of fish angled for, and size of bait and hook used (see page 47). The smaller your bait and hook; the finer your hooklength.

Except when match fishing (see Chapter 17) many anglers prefer to fish with main reel line tied direct to the hook.

Hooklengths are not recommended when fishing for eels, pike or zander (see Chapter 5).

Landing net
Assemble your adjustable long-handled (telescopic) landing net and position the net nearby, preferably close to shallow water beneath the bank.

Hooked!
As soon as you've hooked a fish, begin recovering line. The fish's first instinct is to dive for cover and wrap your line

round underwater obstacles 'til the line snaps or your hook is dislodged. Don't let it happen. Keep a tight line and reel-in. Your bending rod saps the fish's strength.

Try to remain out of sight; make no sudden movement. Stay cool, calm and in control. The instant your hooked fish sees you, he'll panic and surge away with line-snapping power! Ease the fish towards your landing net.

30. An eddy beneath a weir attracts many species of fish, including barbel, chub, perch, pike, roach, trout and zander. Dace and grayling prefer the fast runs.

Using the landing net

When you've hooked a fish, slip your net into the water. A long handle reduces the distance you have to draw the fish before netting and landing – putting the odds in your favour.

As you reel in line, steer the hooked fish over the mouth of your net; then raise the net and land your fish.

Wet your hands

Because fish are cold blooded, the touch of our dry, hot hands burns their flesh just like hot pokers would burn ours. Dry hands also tear away fishes' protective scales – leaving skin exposed to possible infection. Always wet your hands in cooling water before touching a fish to remove your hook from the fish's mouth.

Weighing

Find your fish's weight without causing physical damage to the fish – use a spring-balance and specially designed fish weighing net.

Photographs

Preserve happy fishing memories; impress friends and confound cynics by taking waterside snaps of your best fishes before hurriedly returning them to the water.

To take first-class pictures:

    a) Make sure something appears alongside your fish in the photograph that gives a true impression of size – item of tackle, or this book, ruler etc.

    b) Get the focus right!

    c) Hold the camera steady.

Returning fish

Speedily and gently return your fish to its water, a short distance from the stretch you're fishing. Hold the fish upright (facing into the current in flowing water) until the fish feels strong enough to swim away.

TO CATCH FISH – THINK FISH!

12

BEST GROUNDBAIT
METHODS

Groundbaiting is a ploy to help us catch large numbers of particular fish. Refer to the "Groundbait" entry in each fish's "Fish file", starting on page 16, for details of the fish groundbaiting is most effective in attracting.

Groundbaiting applies to float fishing (see Chapter 14) and legering (see Chapter 15). Groundbaiting is not used when spinning or fly fishing.

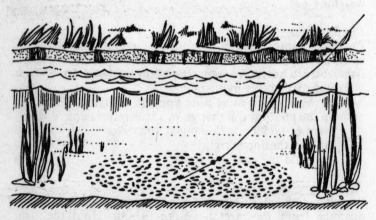

31. Groundbait on the bottom.

Aims of groundbaiting

a) To attract fish to the area of water you are about to fish.

b) To whet the appetite of attracted fish.

c) To offer, mixed with groundbait, small or chopped samples of the larger bait fixed on your hook. This makes fish less suspicious of your hook bait.

d) To encourage attracted fish to stay and continue feeding in the area of water you are fishing.

Types of groundbait

Cloud

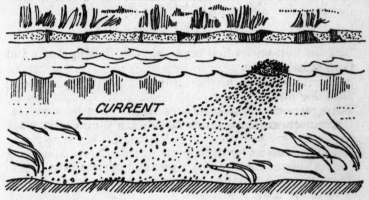

32. "Cloud".

Light, "fluffy" particles designed to fall in a "mysterious", enticing rain through the water from surface to bottom, drawing inquisitive fish to investigate.

Heavy groundbait

33. Heavy groundbait.

Heavier mix, to drop in a ball rapidly through the water and dissolve in a blanket of appetizing morsels on the bottom.

Cloud or heavy?

Cloud
Ideal for shoals of fish feeding close to the surface of clear flowing water and shallow still water.

Heavy
Best for bottom feeding large fish; fast flowing water and deep murky water.

Do's and don'ts
There are no definite do's or don'ts in groundbaiting. Experiment with mixes and methods. Use the ones that work for you!

Tackle dealers stock various groundbaits containing "secret" ingredients, together with full mixing instructions. These are worth trying, but you can also make your own.

Here are some guidelines:

Recipes
CLOUD
Ingredients: stale white bread; egg shells and dry powdered milk.

Method
The amount you make depends on how much cloud you intend using and the proportions of ingredients are variable; but most of the mix should be stale or lightly toasted (not browned or burned) powdered crumbs from white bread (no crust), 85%; a few dried crushed and powdered egg shells, 10%; and a pinch or two of dry powdered milk, 5%.

Save and store these items in an air-tight container as they become available. Then you'll have the mix ready whenever you need some.

Don't add water to the mix until you arrive at your fishing spot. Then tip some water and mix into a round mixing bowl about 127 mm (5 inches) deep. Round bowls are best because no dry patches collect in corners.

Special collapsible bowls are sold by specialist tackle dealers.

At the water's edge
Quiet and crouching low; wash sweat, grease and human smell from your hands. Scoop water into your mixing bowl; sprinkle in some cloud mix. Add chopped or crushed samples of your hook bait (crushed or chopped grubs, maggots, worms or raw meat "bleed" scent and succulent flavour into the water to attract hungry fish). Gently mould into a fluffy *not stodgy* ball, about the size of a golf ball. Make a little at a time, so the mix doesn't dry out.

HEAVY GROUNDBAIT
Ingredients: Stale brown bread and/or toasted "browned" white bread, 75%; bran and/or broken biscuit crumbs, 10%; a small amount of freshly cooked, mashed potato, 10% and/or a pinch or two of semolina powder, 5%.

Method
The quantity you mix depends on the amount of heavy groundbait you want to use and the proportion of ingredients can be varied, but the bulk of mix should be bread (no crust).

Don't put the mix in water until you arrive at the waterside. Then pour some mix into a round mixing bowl about 127 mm (5 inches) deep.

At the water's edge
Keeping quiet and out of the fishes' view; rinse your hands in the water; then scoop water into your mixing bowl; sprinkle in a little heavy groundbait mix. Add chopped or crushed samples of your hook bait. Mould into a *stiff*, "heavy" ball about the size of a tennis ball. For fast flowing water or water over 3.5 m (12 feet) deep, add stones and/or a thin outer casing of mud. Moisten the outside of your heavy groundbait ball with water to seal cracks.

Hints
★ When possible, do your waterside mixing a short way *downstream* (down current) from the spot you intend fishing.
★ Before you throw your mix, select a *target marker* in the water or on the opposite bank (lily pad, stick, tree or bush etc.) so you can cast your baited hook to the same position your groundbait ball entered the water.

★ Throw your ball of cloud or heavy groundbait gently and *low* across the water to avoid a big fish scaring splash!

★ When throwing groundbait or casting line into fast flowing water, reach the spot you want to fish by allowing for the current and throwing or casting slightly upstream (up current).

★ Allow time for your thrown ball of cloud or heavy groundbait to settle on the bottom before casting your baited hook.

★ Special angler's catapults are available for easy and accurate long distance groundbaiting and "feeding" (see below).

Feeding

Having drawn fish to your baited hook; *keep them interested* – there are plenty to catch! Toss a *few small* samples of your hook bait into the water with each fresh cast of your baited hook.

Every 20 to 30 minutes throw another ball of cloud or heavy groundbait, but *never* bigger than a large coin. Leave the fish hungry for your hook bait!

Remember, still shallow, or slow moving waters don't want as much groundbaiting as fast flowing or deep waters. You don't wish to build a mountain of groundbait. Please leave room in the water for fish!

13

CARE FOR YOUR TACKLE

Love your tackle.

Take care of your tackle and it won't let you down when you hook the big one!

Badly maintained tackle may lose you the fish of a lifetime.

Listen to the maker
When you buy new equipment, look for enclosed notes or booklets telling you how to care for the tackle. Read, remember and *do* as the maker advises. He knows best.

While fishing
Rods
Most serious damage to rods occurs while fishing. Don't accidentally tread on a rod section when you're piecing the rod together, or taking it apart.

When dismantling your rod, start by gripping the top end section at the joint (ferrule) and *pull* the rod sections apart. Twisting strains the ferrule fastening. Then work down to the bottom, butt section.

Line
If your line gets snagged, don't strain the rod by pulling; unravel snagged line within easy reach, or gently tug the line free with your hand.

On the move
When walking between trees or bushes with assembled tackle, point the rod behind you; keep the tip low and clear of the ground.

Water's edge
Keep equipment off soil when assembling or dismantling tackle. Protect rod joints (ferrules), rod rings and your reel from unnecessary contact with dirt and grit.

After fishing

As you carefully pack away your tackle at the water's edge; gently wipe the reel; rod sections and rod rings with a soft damp cloth. Check there is no grit or grime on the rod rings, especially the insides; then slip your rod sections into the rod bag.

At home

Examine your tackle for damage or signs of wear and tear. List lost, broken or worn tackle for replacement or repair.

Rods

Remove rod sections from bag; wipe with soft cloth soaked in warm soapy water to remove grease and stains; stand sections in warm to dry. Clean cork handles with a nylon brush or old tooth brush (kept for this purpose) dipped in warm water. When a cork handle gets wet, check it's dry before putting your rod back into the *dry* rod bag.

If rod joints (ferrules) fit too tightly for easy assembly or dismantling, lightly rub them with household soap or a white candle before storing them (unless the maker instructs differently).

Hang rods somewhere cool in rod bags, suspended by the loop provided for this purpose, or stand in a supportive rod rack, or store laid flat in a safe place.

Line

Wind the length of line you estimate you've used for fishing onto an empty bobbin or line spool and wipe the line with a damp cloth; then dry and wind back onto reel. Check the end section of your line for nicks or cuts. If necessary, cut off and discard any length looking worn or limp, stretched and strained. Always cut line; never break off line by snapping, which weakens the line.

Landing nets and keep nets

Wipe landing net handle with damp, soapy cloth. Lightly grease any moving parts. Use special grease supplied for tackle. Check that nuts, bolts and screws tighten properly. Rinse and sponge netting in clean water and leave in warm to dry. Look for holes or tears in mesh. Repair by tying with fine fishing line where possible; replace with new net when badly torn.

Reel

Clean outside of reel with damp cloth; remove any unwanted grease with spirit or cleaning fluid, then dry. Lubricate exterior moving parts monthly with tiny drops of maker's recommended oil. Don't get oil on your line! Keep reel in reel bag, stored in a dry place, away from direct sunlight and extremes of temperature.

Floats

Wipe clean. Replace perished rubber "float caps" (new rubbers available from your tackle dealer).

Hooks

Sharpen used hooks on emery cloth, or special sharpening stone (sold by tackle dealers).

Clean and dry flies, lures, plugs or spinners used. Check that swivels work correctly.

Tackle box

Keep small items of tackle neatly stowed away in a tackle box.

"A place for everything and everything in its place."

Then you know where to find things quickly and without fuss and bother.

Season's end

At the end of your fishing season clean carefully, check and store your tackle, ready for the next fishing year.

Some anglers like to start each season with new line.

Resist the temptation to tinker with the inside parts of reels. If your reel needs attention, pack it securely and post to the maker's service centre. The address is included with your reel's instruction booklet. Don't forget to enclose a letter giving your name, address, telephone number and details of what is wrong with the reel.

Several seasons on

After several seasons your rod may require revarnishing. Use special rod varnish supplied by your tackle dealer.

Chipped or groove-worn rod rings damage lines and need replacing. Buy new rings, whipping thread and rod varnish.

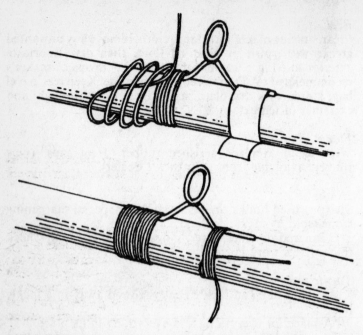

34. Replacing rod rings; how to attach new ones.

To attach new rod rings

a) Remove damaged ring by carefully cutting along old whipping thread with small scissors or sharp tool. Discard old ring and thread.

b) Position new ring precisely and temporarily fasten one end of the ring to rod with sticky tape.

c) Whip the other end of ring onto the rod, as shown above – see fig. 34. Pull thread tight. Cut off loose end of thread. Cut away and discard sticky tape. Whip remaining end of rod ring to rod.

d) Paint thin layer of varnish on whippings with clean brush.

e) Smooth varnished whippings with clean piece of cloth.

f) Apply another coat of varnish; smooth with cloth; then put rod somewhere warm and dust-free to dry.

14

FLOAT FISHING

Float fishing is skilful and exciting. Few sporting thrills compare to the heart-throbbing moment your float quivers with life as a fish bites your baited hook.

The right rod
A long rod between 3.35 m (11 ft) to 4 m (13 ft) is advisable for float fishing. The longer your rod: a) the more easily you may fish well back from the waterside – staying hidden from the fishes' sight; b) the further you can cast light lines and floats; c) the greater your control over the "natural" presentation of float fished bait; d) the quicker you can tighten and reel-in line when your float indicates you've hooked a fish.

Floats are for:
a) Indicating when a fish is investigating, nibbling or swallowing your bait.

b) Suspending your bait at the precise depth you expect the fish to be feeding.

c) Giving you delicate control over the drift, position and presentation of your baited hook.

d) Keeping your bait above muddy, leafy, weedy water bottoms; obstacles and snags.

e) Enabling you to float and present your bait, in a natural way, to fish-infested stretches of water beyond casting distance; overhung by branches or bushes, or otherwise inaccessible.

Types
Floats are made in many sizes, weights and styles. In general, floats with their main buoyancy ("fatness") near the top are designed for maximum effectiveness on fast and medium-fast flowing water; floats with their main buoyancy ("fatness") near the bottom are especially effective on slow

moving and still water. Despite the numerous names, there are basically 2 types of float.

1. Stick floats and balsas

These floats are fastened to your line at the top and bottom ends and designed for fishing fast and medium-fast *flowing* waters.

*** TIME SAVER ***

For quick and easy float change (useful when competition match fishing, see Chapter 17); attach stick floats and balsas top and bottom to the line with *two* rubber rings (float caps). Then you don't have to thread line through the float's bottom eye, and "instant" float changes are possible.

2. Wagglers (including missiles, antennas, duckers etc.).

Specially designed to fish *still* and *slow moving* waters. These floats attach to your line through their bottom eye only and can be kept in place by weights fastened on the line at both sides of the float's eye (see below, fig 35).

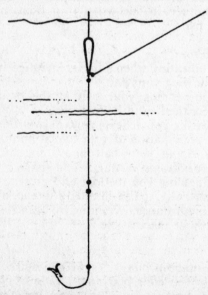

35. How to attach a waggler.

Pointers to success

To achieve maximum success float fishing, take note of these points:

a) Quietly and without undue disturbance, plumb the depth (see page 64) of the stretch of water you are about to fish.

b) Decide at what depth the fish you're after are probably feeding (see "Fish file", Chapter 5) and how much line to allow between your float and the hook to reach the correct "feeding" depth.

c) Always select the smallest and lightest float that suits the water you're fishing, so fish feel minimum resistance on the line when they examine your bait. Fast flowing waters, long casts, heavy baits and strong winds may dictate use of heavier floats.

d) Choose a float with its top painted a colour *you* can see best at a distance. Different colours stand out well against particular backgrounds and in different light conditions. But our eyes vary in the colours most readily picked up – you'll have to experiment.

Easily spotted float top colours include: black, orange, red, white and yellow.

Make sure the underside of your float is white or a drab, mottled camouflage colour. We don't want the fish dazzled!

e) Aim to fix as few weights as possible on your line when float fishing. Fish feel the unnatural pull of each weight when they tug your bait. Some weight is usually necessary to "cock" your float (make it float upright). When correctly cocked, only the tip of your float should be visible.

f) Sometimes the weight of your baited hook alone is sufficient to cock the float and addition of weights to your line may be unnecessary.

g) Self-cocking floats are marketed and give good casting performance without added weights.

h) Weights might be necessary to sink your bait quickly in fast flowing water. Never bunch weights too close together; space them out and decrease the size as you near the hook, then your bait rises and falls naturally in the current; offering minimal resistance to suspicious fish.

i) If your float instantly disappears under the water when cast, you've either hooked a fish or, more probably, put too many weights on your line. Remedy: take off some weights – or use a bigger float!

j) For long casts without excessive weighting of your line, mould mud or groundbait around one of the weights on the line, or your hook bait; then cast. The extra weight of mud or groundbait carries your bait the right distance and falls loose on impact with the water.

k) Don't cast long distances, or fish your float far away without good reason. The further your float from the rod tip, the less control you have over presentation of your bait, and the more delay tightening and reeling-in hooked fish. Any delay in landing a hooked fish favours the fish's chance of escape!

l) When fish fail to show interest in your float-fished bait;

    1. Change the bait.
    2. Alter the depth you're fishing by adjusting the float.
    3. Remove, add or reposition the weights on your line.
    4. Don't resort to your "lucky" float in moments of despair. Look, think, then adapt your tackle, bait and approach according to your *reasoned* assessment of the situation.

      When all else fails . . . there's always your lucky float!

m) Keep the line between rod tip and float taut and *off* the water (see below, fig 36). *Unless*, the water is unusually choppy and you're float fishing with the line fixed only to the bottom eye of your float by two weights (see page 78, fig 35); in which case place the rod tip slightly *below* the water surface and reel the line tight. This action reduces the transmission of disturbing vibrations to your hook bait.

Bites

When a fish has taken your hook bait into its mouth and you have a "bite", you should straightaway tighten the line to drive your hook firmly into the fish's lip.

    Your float indicates a "bite" by:

    1. Not standing upright in the water after being cast (immediate bite by fish).
    2. Quivering in the water.
    3. Disappearing under the water.
    4. Lifting out of the water.
    5. Rising slightly, then laying flat on the water.
    6. Moving across the water, against the current.

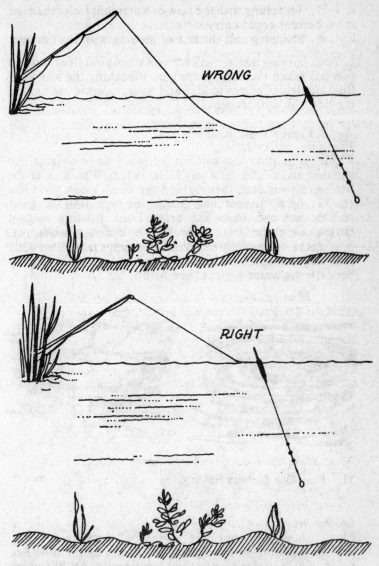

36. Keep the line between rod tip and float taut.
(Above): The *wrong* way. The line between the rod tip and
float is not taut.
(Below): The *right* way.

7. Travelling with the flow of water, but faster than the current could carry it.

8. Stopping still instead of moving with the current.

Your hunting instinct will tell you when your float shows a fish has taken the bait. There's no mistaking the way your float suddenly "comes to life" and your response – to tighten the line – is instantaneous.

A – Z Float fishing methods
Free-line surface fishing
Fishing a floating bait without using a float or weights! An exciting and challenging way to hook fish. Watch to see the fish seize your bait, then tighten the line. Grease your line (buy some fly fishers' line grease, see page 100) for good results, and fish baits like bread crust, floating maggot chrysalis ("caster", see page 48), housefly, grasshopper, beetle etc., or carefully cast your line so it drapes over a lily pad and daintily dangle the hook bait (any bait) slightly beneath the water surface. See below, fig 37.

37. Free-line surface fishing.

Laying-on
Float fishing with your bait "laying on" the water bottom; held in position by a weight fixed firmly to the line. See below, fig 38. Refer also to float legering on page 88 (where the leger weight is attached but not "fixed" to the line – which is free to run through the leger weight).

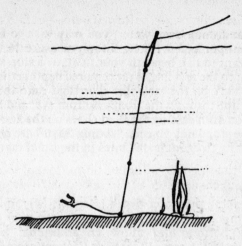

38.   Laying-on.

Off-bottom float fishing
Standard float fishing practice. Suspend your bait "off-bottom" at a pre-selected depth. See below, fig 39.

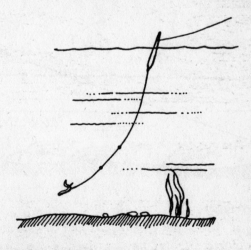

39.   Off-bottom float fishing.

Sliding float
When float fishing deep water, you may wish to fish your
bait deeper than 3.65 m (12 ft). Simply measure the length of
line you want to fish beneath your float; tie a stop knot (see
page 57) onto the reel line at the required depth setting; wind
your line back on the reel; slip your float onto the line by
threading line through the float's bottom eye, and leave the
float free, so after casting the float slides up the line until it's
held by the stop knot. Special "sliding floats" are marketed.

The sliding float indicates bites in the usual manner (see
page 80).

Stret-pegging
After plumbing the water depth (see page 64), adjust your
float to support enough line for your baited hook to reach
the water bottom *and* allow an additional length of
approximately 305 mm (12 inches). Cast your line. Keeping
the rod tip low and pointing towards the water, hold your
float stationary. Make sure that when the line between rod
tip and float is taut the line's off the water surface. Your
baited hook rises, falls and wavers in the current fractionally
above the water bottom (see below, fig 40).

When you want to fish a different stretch of water; reel-in
and re-cast.

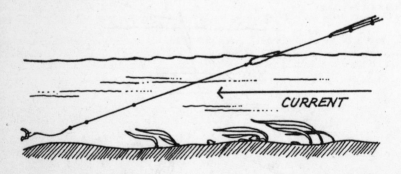

40. Stret-pegging.

Trotting (also known as "long-trotting" and "swimming the
stream").
Feeding out line, allow your float to carry the baited hook

in natural fashion with the flow of the current for distances up to 30 m (98 ft) or until the float can't be seen, or fairly swift tightening of the line becomes impractical. Useful method for fishing otherwise inaccessible spots, and tempting shy or suspicious fish, while staying hidden beyond their sight and hopefully, hearing.

15

LEGERING

Legering is fishing with your bait anchored in position on or near the bottom of the water by a weight or weights.

Some advantages
a) You can cast far from the bank with a heavily weighted line. The heavier the weight, the further out you may fish. A 15 g (½ oz) weight carries your baited hook up to 55 m (60 yds); a 21 g (¾ oz) weight to 73 m (80 yds).
b) A bait anchored at the bottom of fast flowing water often fascinates fish and proves a sure way to make big catches.
c) Large fish frequently lie in hiding at the bottom of deep water and are easily reached by legering.
d) Clear patches at the bottom of heavily weeded, reeded; branch- or root-cluttered water can be fished with precision, without worrying too much about getting your line snagged on submerged obstacles.

Leger tackle
A sturdy rod 2.75 m (9 ft) or 3 m (10 ft) in length is ideal. Use a slightly stronger line than you would normally, to allow for shock and strain caused by casting a heavy leger weight. The heavier the weight, the stronger your line must be.

Tackling up
    1. Always use the lightest leger weight necessary to:
    a) Cast the distance you want to achieve.
    b) Keep your baited hook on or near the bottom.
    2. When fishing stillwaters without below surface currents, you probably need no leger weight whatever; simply allow your bait to sink naturally and settle life-like on the bottom.
    3. The closer a weight to your bait, the less rise and fall of the baited hook in any current, and the more obviously a trap to clever fish. Try to leave about 152 mm (6 inches) to 457 mm (18 inches) of unweighted

free-drifting line between hook bait and the nearest weight.

To hold your baited hook on or near the water bottom in strong currents, the leger weight should be close to the bait.

Handy hints
Before fishing
a) Select the stretch of water likely to hold the best fish; choose the exact spot you want to place your baited hook.
b) Scan water for visible signs of submerged obstacles; note position of weed beds.
c) Check the depth of the area of water you intend fishing by plumbing (see page 64). Gently reel in line; feeling for sudden tautness indicating underwater snags. Look for pieces of weed caught around the plumbing weight – warning of the presence of heavy weed.
d) Expect gradual drift in leger weight and bait position when fishing in a strong current. A leger weight of 42 g (1½ oz) might be required to anchor your baited hook in very fast flowing water.

*** TIP ***
Groundbait (see Chapter 12) firmly balled around your leger weight gives added distance to your cast and supplies a bonus attraction for fish as it fans out and settles seductively close to your baited hook.

Detecting bites
To detect bites when leger fishing without a float, you can buy easily-attached sensitive rod tip or rod butt swinging bite indicators that fit most rods.

Super-sensitive electronic bite indicators, fitted onto bank sticks (rod rest supports) are useful for daytime and night-time legering.

Also effective as a bite indicator, is a lump of bread paste or piece of silver paper (or white-painted cork, split down the centre) pinched onto loose hung line (see below, fig 41). Movement of the paste or paper shows a bite.

A float may be used as a bite indicator when legering (see page 90, fig 43 and page 91, fig 45). Pick the smallest, slimmest float you can see without straining your eyes (see Chapter 14, page 79).

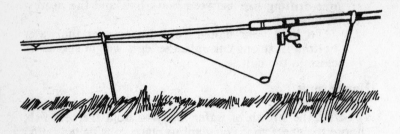

41. An effective home-made bite indicator.

Touch legering is a sensitive, thrilling and skilful way of detecting bites. Keep your rod pointing steadily downwards towards the bait. With line taut; grip the line in front of your reel gently between thumb and forefinger, and wait to feel unmistakable sharp tugs, snatches, twitches or tremors that telegraph the fish's bite through your line preceding a run with the bait; tighten... and the fight is on!

Leger weight guide-lines
Here are some examples of successful ways to set up lines for legering. These are guides; your own experimental and tested adaptations and modifications should work just as well.

The tiny "stop" weight placed in front of the heavier free-running leger weight, prevents the leger moving too near your hook; at the same time allowing curious and suspicious fish to examine and swim away with your baited hook without immediately feeling resistance from the heavy leger weight. Another small "stop" weight may be attached about 457 mm (18 inches) above the leger weight to prevent the leger weight working its way too far up the line in a rolling current.

A – Z legering methods
Float legering
Attach a small, slender float to your line; keep your line tight and off the water, unless the surface is especially choppy (see page 80, letter (m)). Bites are usually indicated by your float quivering and/or disappearing under the water, but watch also for other unexpected or "unnatural" movements of your float, which might show a bite (see page 80).

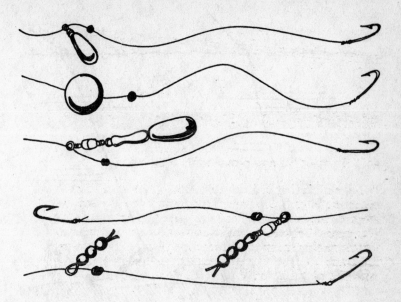

42. Five ways of setting up a line for legering.

a) Bomb or pear shape leger weight.
b) Pierced ball or "bullet" shape leger weight.
c) Bomb or pear shape leger weight clipped onto link swivel.
d) Link leger – easily made (see page 91), attached to swivel on line.
e) Link leger – easily made (see page 91), attached direct to line.

Free-line legering
Allow the baited hook to sink slowly and naturally without any weight or float attached. Ideal in still or slow moving water. Move rod tip to influence direction of bait's "natural" drift.

Legered floating bait
A light, naturally floating bait (like bread crust) may be held in position by a leger weight (see over, fig 44).

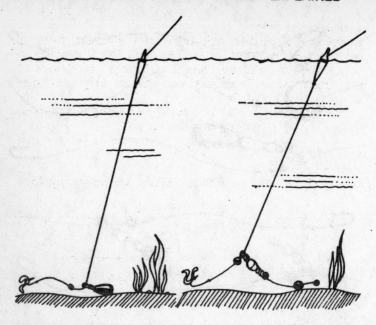

43. **Float legering.**

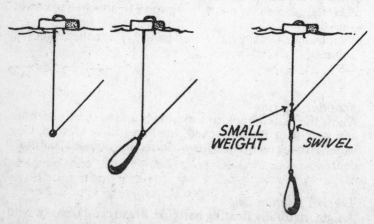

SMALL
WEIGHT

SWIVEL

44. **A legered floating bait.**

Link legering
Convenient, speedily adjustable and effective form of legering, see page 89, fig 42. The "link leger" is made by fixing weights on a short length of looped line. This is an inexpensive way of making your own leger weights at home or on the bankside.

The total weight may be altered by adding or removing single weights of similar or differing size.

Paternoster
Can be fished with or without a float, see below, fig 45.

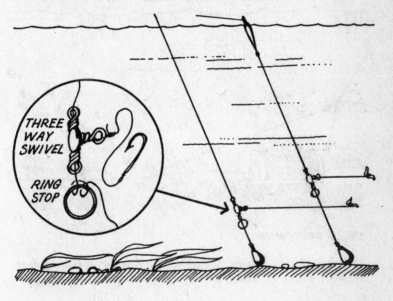

THREE WAY SWIVEL

RING STOP

45. A paternoster.

Keeps your bait stationary above weed beds and underwater snags. Fix a 3 way swivel. An easily attached and adjustable smooth split ring "stop" saves trying unnecessary line-weakening knots to fasten the swivel to your rod line.

Swimfeeder
A swimfeeder does the job of a leger weight *and* deposits an

attracting stream of groundbait or feed (see Chapter 12) near your hook bait.

Simply fill the swimfeeder with tasty scraps and cast.

Regular 10 to 20 minute rewinding of the swimfeeder; refilling and recasting keeps shoals of fish feeding keenly and can lead to large catches.

Swimfeeders come in various designs, weights and sizes, and may be set up in different ways. Experiment to find your favourite design and style of use.

46. A swimfeeder.

Extra weight can be added to the line when fishing fast flowing water or where an especially long cast is desired.

Upstream legering
Very effective in shallow water running with strong currents.

The link leger (see page 89, fig 42) is best for this type of fishing. Cast the baited hook upstream (up current) and let the current slowly roll the legered bait to your feet. Then repeat the action. Encourage continuous motion of the bait by occasional reeling-in. Don't pull your bait out of the water the minute it reaches you – careful fish follow awhile, then snatch and run at the last moment!

16

UP THE POLE

The increasingly popular pole is no newcomer to the U.K. Although now mainly associated with Continental fishermen, the pole was fished in parts of England many years past, and only slipped out of use in the early 1900's.

Fully extended, today's poles range in length from round 3 m (10 feet) to 9.5 m (31 feet). Given ideal conditions, the splendid pole can catch far more small fish at close range than could rod and line.

The pole often proves a match winner!

The pole's many attractive features include:

*Line attached directly to pole end, therefore no reel or reeling-in to bother you and eat up valuable match fishing time. Simply swing hooked small fish into your hand, or large fish into a long-handled landing net.

* Line shock absorbers built in and/or attached to the pole, mean you may fish almost invisibly fine lines of 227 g (8 oz) breaking strain and land fish of 1 Kg (2¼ lbs) in weight.

*Your pole can be extended to drop a lightly weighted line and hook bait gently, without splash or scary noise – up to 9.5 m (31 feet) away.

* From safe cover far back on the bankside, you can thoroughly fish the water in front of you, before approaching the water's edge and fishing across towards the opposite bank.

* Because your float may be fished less than a metre (3 feet) from the pole end, you have total control over the "natural" presentation of the hook bait and should really fool fish.

*No casting necessary, so no more nasty tangles!

* You have direct contact with hooked fish, which don't have slack line to run with and can't escape by snagging your line in weed or submerged obstacles.

*Replacement lines, complete with pre-selected float, weights and hook, are wound on clearly labelled special line winders by you at home and neatly connected to the pole end when fishing. This saves fiddling, time-consuming water's edge tackle changes.

*You can fish into strong winds that would make conventional rod and reel float fishing extremely difficult.

Disadvantages
1. You can't fish much beyond 9.5 m (31 feet).
2. You'll get "smashed" by BIG fish.
3. You'll soon tire of holding the pole, *unless* you hold it properly.

Pole holding

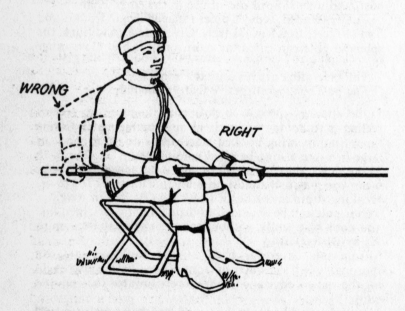

47. How to hold the pole.
Left: Wrong. Body muscles not relaxed.
Right: Correct. Weight of pole balanced by left arm. Knee acting as a pole-rest and pivot. Body relaxed.

17

WIN MATCHES

To *win* matches you must acquire knowledge, experience and skill; develop confidence and be highly competitive. You must will yourself to win. Firstly, you *need* the help, support and encouragement of a good fishing club.

Join a club
Fish in club and club team matches. Check angling press for details of "Open" (open to all) matches; enter or watch as many as you can. Most open matches require early payment of entrance fee – check date deadlines; book early.

Watch others fish in competitions, see what tackle and methods they use. Note any special tackle and tricks employed by winners. Don't be afraid to ask for tips and advice, *after* the fishing is finished! Read angling newspapers, magazines and books. Keep up-to-date with tackle developments and fishing techniques.

Visit venues
Before fishing in a match, try to visit the water. Watch the local club team fish; chat to club members – watch, listen and get the "feel" of the water. Study the water – make notes. For instance: which "pegs" (pegged and numbered bankside match positions, see over, fig 48) are likely to produce which species and size of fish? What special snags and advantages does each peg offer? Which baits usually produce best results in what particular weather and water conditions? Should you try for a winning weight of small fish, or win with fewer heavy fish?

Specialize
Specialize in your local waters. You can easily practise and perfect your methods and you should aim to become unbeatable in your "home" matches.

48.   Match fishing "peg".

Before the match

Plan your strategy: what weight of fish will you probably need to win? Which species will you catch to make this weight? What methods and tackle should produce winning results? Check match rules for banned baits – wasp grubs, hempseed etc.

Sort out your tactics: what breaking strain line/lines, hook baits, groundbait, hooks and floats will you use? And in what order of precedence?

Aim to keep time-consuming changes to a minimum. Time cost is fish lost!

Practise your match methods.

Be prepared to scrap ideas and re-think your approach. Never get stuck in a rut. The right method is the one that wins!

Day before match find out probable weather and water conditions. If necessary, amend plans accordingly.

Check all tackle is in A1 condition. Put new line on reel if necessary; sharpen hooks; securely tie hooks to hooklength line (see page 64).

Get a good night's sleep.

On match day collect bait; keep bait cool and fresh. RELAX. Remain cool, calm and confident. Your careful preparation should win the match.

Fingers crossed for a little luck at the peg draw. Be prepared for a long hike to your peg – never pack unnecessary equipment. Don't let spectators affect your calm, confident approach. You are there to enjoy yourself.

At your peg, lay out assembled tackle and bait *neatly* and within easy reach. Take your time, "more haste, less speed". When permitted, plumb depths (see page 64); pick best spots to begin fishing. It's often best to begin by *lightly* ground-baiting near the bank; fish caught can be quickly unhooked and keep-netted. If you've no bite within 5 minutes, change your hook bait. Lightly groundbait at 10 to 15 minute intervals; reduce groundbaiting as bites increase. Reduce groundbaiting further as bites become less frequent – the fish are stuffing themselves with your groundbait!

Concentrate on drawing fish into a small, easily fished area. Allow an unfished "safe zone" to develop at a convenient spot in your stretch of water where frightened fish feel secure. Don't scare them into your neighbour's peg! You can catch all "safe zone" fish near the end of the match.

Expect nearby experienced competitors to try tricking you into making foolish moves that could cost you the match. Watch for feigned heavy groundbaiting or "feeding" (see page 72); mock hook baiting (is that large container of maggots or sweetcorn really being used, or merely a blind?). Keep an eye on anglers doing well, but don't be panicked into changing your plans and copying their temporarily successful techniques. In an hour they'll be copying you!

Don't dwell on mistakes; be positive and believe in yourself. Your painstaking practice rewards you with an automatic skill that coasts you to victory.

After the match has finished *check* your catch weight on the scales at weigh-in, then immediately and gently return fish to their water.

Keep smiling. You could be the next World Champion!

18

FLY FISHING FOR FRESHWATER FISH

Many freshwater fish may be caught by fishing an artificial fly.

Fly fishing, although mainly associated with the sporting pursuit of salmon, trout and grayling, can also be a fruitful way of catching barbel, bream, carp, chub, dace, perch, roach and rudd. Even large pike and eels have been hooked on flies.

Fish feed on the most abundant and easiest-to-catch form of food. From May to September clouds of flies hatch and rise from the water; presenting fish with a feast which few can resist.

Ephemeridae
The family of insects known as "ephemeridae" includes the flies: Blue Dun, Olive Dun, Iron Blue, March Brown, Pale Watery Dun, Mayfly and Blue Winged Olive.

The life-cycle of the ephemeridae is worth examining to broaden our understanding of the appeal that artificial flies have for fish.

The beautiful flies of the ephemeridae family begin life when they hatch as NYMPHS from eggs laid in the water. The underwater life of the different nymphs lasts from one to two years. In summer the fully developed nymph swims to the surface; the case splits and the fly emerges to dry its wings in the warm air. During this phase it is known as a DUN. With wings dried, the dun flies to the bank; sheds its skin – is now termed a SPINNER, and in final winged magnificence finds a mate. The mated female lays her eggs on the water surface. After mating and egg laying the flies die; their bodies drift on the water. At this stage the dead flies are called SPENT SPINNERS. The life-cycle from emerging "dun" to "spent spinner" is usually over in a few days; during warm weather the cycle is sometimes completed within 24 hours!

In addition to the ephemeridae, there are other flies of great value to the fly fisher including the Alder; sedge flies (whose larvae are caddis grubs); gnats, midges (bloodworms are midge larvae) and stone-flies. And we mustn't forget crane-flies, hawthorn flies and flying ants – all of which have their commercially available artificial imitators.

Dry fly fishing
Dry fly fishing presents fish with floating artificial imitations of duns, spinners, spent spinners and other insects.

Wet fly fishing
Wet fly fishing offers fish sunken artificial flies and insects (nymphs, grubs, beetles, shrimps, snails, tiny fish fry etc.).

Flashers
Both wet and dry fly fishers may make use of "flashers" or "attractors", that resemble no known insects, but which excite and entice fish to snatch them.

Hook size
Artificial flies range in size from a tiny midge on small hook size 18 to an "attractor" on large hook size 8 and include 102 mm (4 inch) weighted tube flies to fish near the bottom of fast flowing water for big fish.

Tackle
Balanced tackle is essential to fly fishers for efficient and accurate casting; effective control and natural presentation of the artificial fly in water, and landing the hooked fish.
    Always ask your specialist tackle dealer for advice when selecting fly fishing tackle.

Rods and reels
A 2.6 m (8½ ft) fly rod is a good buy for beginners. Your reel is best light but strongly constructed.

Lines
Lines for fly fishing must be matched to the rod used. Fly lines carry an AFTM number (Association of Fishing Tackle Manufacturers) and this number should match the AFTM number recommended for your rod.
    Because the fly you cast has little weight, distance is

achieved by the weight of your tapered fly line. A double tapered line is tapered at both ends of its length and can be reversed on your reel when one regularly-fished tapered end is reduced through normal cutting, breakage and trimming.

Fly lines are about 27.4 m to 32 m (30 yds to 35 yds) long and need tying (see page 58) to at least 45.7 m (50 yds) of strong *backing line* to fill the reel and allow spare line for long, line-stripping sprints by big fish.

Don't use white or brightly coloured fly lines – these flash warning signals to the fish. For best results buy dark coloured lines.

Leaders

A "leader" is the link between fly line and artificial fly. Your leader should be about 2.7 m (3 yds) long and made from line with a breaking strain of 1.1 Kg (2½ lbs) or more, depending on the size of fly you're fishing and balance of tackle. Use fine, low breaking-strain leaders for small flies. Fish notice heavy leader line roped to a fragile fly!

A tapered leader is best for dry fly fishing.

Experienced wet fly fishers may use 2 or 3 flies on a leader. One fly on the leader tip, called the "point fly"; one in the middle, the "middle dropper" and the fly nearest your rod, the "top dropper". The middle dropper and top dropper are attached to the main leader by "dropper" lines extending not more than 76 mm (3 inches) from the main leader line.

Inexperienced wet fly fishers should stick to the one end-of-leader "point fly" until they feel they could cope with catching two or maybe three fish simultaneously!

Accessories

Other necessary items of equipment include: special fly fishers' grease to help line float; de-greasing agents to encourage quick sinking of leader lines and/or removal of unwanted line grease; oils, sprays and chemical compounds to assist dry flies to float; wet flies to sink, and clean and recondition all artificial flies between catches or before storing the flies in your flybox or wallet.

Casting

Casting a fly line isn't difficult. Correctly cast, your rod and line do the work; powering your artificial fly to the precise point you want to place it.

For casting expertise, take tuition from an expert caster. Fishing clubs, some local councils and private courses offer excellent practical instruction from basic to advanced levels.

Meanwhile, practice helps make perfect!

Get to grips

First, get the right grip – comfortable and firm. See below, fig 49.

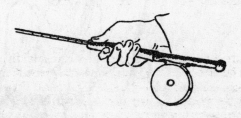

49.   The right hold for a fly rod.

Next, look round to check all's clear – no trees, bushes or people. Stand comfortably. Strip and loop a metre or more of line from your reel. See over, fig 50.

Using your forearm and with a final flick of the wrist, bring your rod vertically upright so the length of line at the rod tip straightens out behind – parallel to the ground; bending the rod tip. This is called the *back cast* (see page 103, fig 51 (i)). Then bring the rod forwards, in the *forward cast* (see page 103, fig 51 (ii)). If the line cracks like a whip, you've brought it forwards too soon – before the line was fully extended behind you. Release the looped line held near your reel. When the fig 51 (iii) position is reached the downwards movement of your rod is halted and the fly gently alights on the water.

Timing and rhythm come with practice.

*** TIP ***

Don't cast just for the sake of casting. If you can crawl close to feeding fish and quietly plop your fly in front of them, without having to make a normal cast – do so!

50. Preparing to cast a fly.

Flies
There are dozens of artificial fly patterns to choose from.
However, your confidence and skilful presentation of any fly
frequently brings success, irrespective of the fly fished.

Ask local advice about choice of artificial fly before
fishing. Effectiveness of individual flies varies from locality
to locality and from week-to-week (even day-to-day),
depending on insect activity and the feeding whims and
fancy of fish.

Coachman, Ginger Quill and Greenwell's Glory (fished
dry) are successful dry flies on many trout waters.

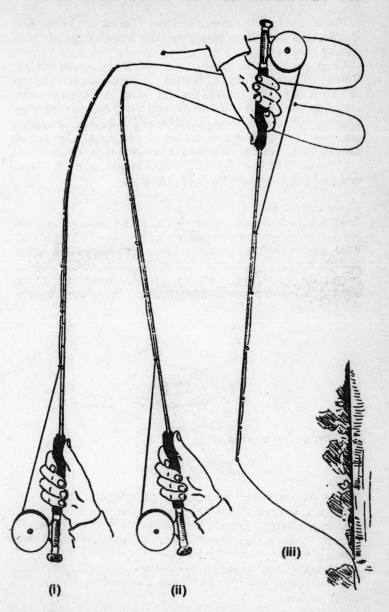

(i)   (ii)   (iii)

51.   The cast in progress.

Black Spider, Greenwell's Glory (fished wet) and Red Palmer are wet flies that generally produce good trout fishing results.

Carp, chub, barbel and perch can be taken on Alexander, Butcher, Palmer, Zulu etc. Bream, dace, roach and rudd fall to Black Gnat, Coch-Y-Bonddu, Wickham's Fancy etc. Grayling seize most small artificial trout flies, but especially alluring are: Tup's Indispensable and Red Tag (a special grayling fly). Eels snatch sea trout flies and pike pursue salmon flies. For big eels or pike attach a large fly and level leader line of at least 6.8 Kg (15 lbs.) breaking strain – large eels and pike can bite through fine line.

Detecting bites
Keep line taut as possible between fly and rod tip. Once the fish has tasted your artificial fly, the fly will soon be spat out. You haven't any time to waste. Look for a fish snatching the fly; feel for tugs or tremors; watch line on water for sudden movement – curling, running, straightening etc; or an unexpected stop in motion. In all cases immediately tighten the line and hook your fish.

19

SPINNING SPORT

Thrill to the hunt for bream, chub, grayling, perch, pike, roach, trout and zander by luring them to snap at spinning or diving artificial baits; enjoy the exciting feel of the fish's fierce strike, and the exhilaration of playing and landing the fish.

Balance tackle
Light and powerful specialized spinning rods, range in length from about 1.82 m (6 ft) to 2.74 m (9 ft); for maximum comfort and ease of casting, carefully balance your tackle by selecting reel and line that suit the rod. Your specialist tackle dealer will be pleased to advise you.

On the move
Spinning offers great sport. Travelling light; constantly moving from one likely spot to another keeps us active, athletic and warm in winter. And you can cover a lot of water in a short time.

Lures
Lures, or artificial baits for spinning, come in many different shapes and sizes; they include fly spoons, spoons, minnows and plugs.

Small fly spoons and ordinary wobbling spoons are often deadly attractive to bream, chub, grayling, perch and roach; trout and zander rarely resist a well spun minnow: pike are frequently taken on plugs. But there are no rules and enticingly presented lures attract cannibal fish of all species.

The size of water you fish suggests your choice of lure. Big waters hide the biggest fish. So choose small spinners for streams and larger lures for rivers, ponds, lakes and lochs.

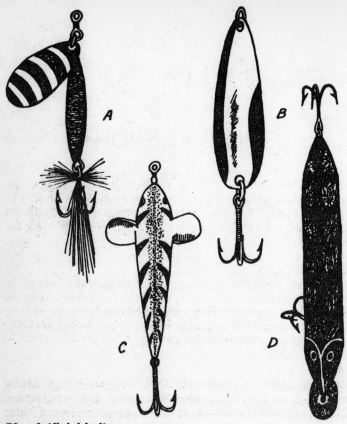

52. Artficial baits
(A) Fly spoon.
(B) Spoon.
(C) Devon minnow.
(D) Plug.

Swivel and anti-kink
To be sure of preventing kinks and tangles sometimes caused in your line by your lure's spinning, attach a swivel and/ or an anti-kink vane (or anti-kink weight) to the line, see below, fig 53.

Selective spinning
Carefully select the spot you spin. Look for large fishes'

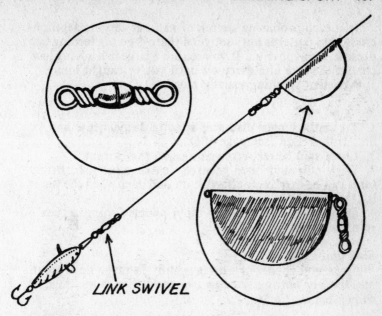

LINK SWIVEL

53. An anti-kink spinning vane and swivel.
Use either or both along your line. The link swivel (to clip a change of lure onto your line quickly) is optional; you may tie the lure direct to the line.

likely hideaways; quietly plumb the water (see page 64) or guess the depth. Eye water for weeds and underwater obstructions which could snag your spinner or plug and snap the line. The more hooks attached to your lure the greater your chance of losing the lure. Cast low over the water and accurately, to avoid excessive fish-scaring splash. Begin rewinding line as the lure slips into the water; keep line tight – skilfully vary speed of reeling; alter rod tip angle. Breathe life into your lure through the connecting line by making the lure rise, weave, dip and dive like a wounded fish – just off bottom and temptingly close to the monster fish's lurking place. Bring your line to the bank's edge before removing the lure from the water: often a cannibal fish follows, strikes and seizes its prey at the very last second.

So fierce is the fish's seizure of a lure that tightening the line to drive hooks home is unnecessary and you'll have no doubt your fish is hooked by the strain on your rod and line.

Spin each promising stretch of water at varying depths in criss-cross patterns until satisfied there is no big feeding fish present, then move on. If you're sure a large fish is lying low, change the lure and carry on until you've caught him.

Persistent spinning usually pays.

*** TIPS ***
1. To cast a longer distance, attach a heavier lure and/or anti-kink weight (see page 106).
2. Lures spin better retrieved *against* the current.
3. Dark coloured lures generally catch most fish. Bright lures can be extremely effective on dull days when the water is clouded.
4. Don't spin water close to other people fishing, or you'll ruin their sport.

Sink and draw

Big pike and zander can be caught by fishing a dead sprat, mackerel or herring fixed to *two treble* hooks and line, as shown below, fig 54.

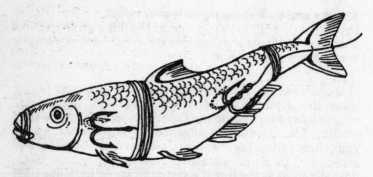

54.   Preparing a dead sprat, mackerel or herring for sink and draw.

Bind or sew the mouth shut. Puncture the fish with a sharp knife before casting, to be certain it sinks; then slowly reel back the line as you would when spinning; raise and lower the rod tip to sink your bait to the water bottom; then draw the bait towards the surface in a series of jerky movements; make the dead fish appear frantic and distressed. Pull the line tight when you feel the bait seized, then the fight is on . . .

20

TOP TWENTY
TROUT TIPS

1. In fast flowing streams fish for trout behind large submerged stones, roots or clumps of weed; in bank undercuts or hollows; where a rapid flow meets calm or shallow water.

2. Big trout prefer deep pools in streams and rivers during daytime, moving into shallows to feed at night.

3. Trout like regular feeding spots; facing into the current when in moving water. Find these spots; creep behind the feeding trout from downstream (down current) and cast your line ahead of the trout, so your bait drifts towards him.

4. Trout queue according to size for food in the best feeding spots. Monster trout always take top place. Find ace feeding spots and catch big trout first, then the smaller ones!

5. Good size trout can be caught under bridges, where they lie for safety, shade and the regular supply of insects tumbling from supports.

6. Small streams, ditches and rivulets of water carry insects into the main river, stream or lake and this attracts trout. Fish for big trout where the waters meet.

7. You often find trout in the swirling water of eddies, where fish find food easily.

8. Deep pools below weirs and waterfalls provide safe, popular places for trout to hide and feed.

9. Stillwater lake, loch and reservoir trout frequently feed in shallow water near the bank because these are breeding areas for insects.

10. When fishing stillwater lochs, lakes or reservoirs in a strong wind, fish with the wind behind you. Trout gather to snap insects blown from the bank. Trout in stillwater move fair distances in their search for food.

11. Trout living in a river or stream in flood move close to the bank to escape strong currents and feed on insects washed into the water.

12. Take advantage of large chunks of bankside newly collapsed into water. Trout will be attracted to the area by wriggling insects washed from the mud.

13. To track trout, look and listen for:

a) Rush of minnows scattering for cover in shallow water.

b) Sudden splashes, ripples, waves or spreading rings on water surface.

14. Watch for kingfishers and herons. They know where small fish are. Big trout won't be far away.

Birds snatching insects over water show you where flies are hatching. Trout will be there too.

15. Trout in all waters keep well under the surface in very hot or cold weather. To catch them, fish deep shaded areas of water.

16. On hot summer days trout often feed fast and furiously early morning (dawn) and late evening (sunset). Monster trout may start feeding near sunset and continue into the night.

17. Search for pools and stretches of water hidden from view by bushes and dense undergrowth. These spots are seldom fished and often hide big trout.

18. Wear polarised sun-glasses to see trout hidden by glare from light reflected off water. Then fish for trout where you find them.

19. When you can see a trout which doesn't seem to be feeding and repeatedly refuses to take your bait; keep trying – trout often seize any object that keeps annoying them.

20. For top trout catches specialize. Concentrate on one or two waters for a whole season; try somewhere new next season. Learn the trout feeding patterns; favourite foods and secret hiding places. Know a water well and catch trout by skill. Don't rely on uncertain "luck".

21

HOW TO HUNT
BIG FISH

Anyone can hunt big fish, few catch them.

Qualities you need
Wide practical experience of fishing; knowledge and understanding of traditional and modern theory and practice, and, more important, a sympathetic awareness of how and why fish behave as they do, combined with an ability to predict correctly fish movement and feeding patterns.

You must be keen, skilful, confident, dedicated and patient. Above all, you need luck!

Secret service
Start your own secret service agency today. Gathering fishing intelligence is vital for catching BIG fish.

Keep a separate file on each species of fish you are interested in pursuing. Record details of waters where big fish have been and are being, caught. Note date, baits and tackle used by captor; time of day or night fished; weather conditions and water temperature (if known). Was groundbait used? If so, what mix? Trawl information from fishing papers, magazines and books; T.V. and local radio.

Check maps for likely locations of "secret" waters yielding big fish referred to by fishermen or the media. Listen to anglers' gossip – jot down stories about monster fish sighted or hooked and lost. Trace the water's owner – individual, club, syndicate or "free" and if applicable, ask for details of licence and/or ticket fees, membership application, water rules and regulations.

Method is a must
Work begins once you've found a water holding big fish of the species you are hunting.

Methodical approach and preparation is essential to

success. Before you dip baited hook in water check, record and map (with the aid of polarised sun-glasses, line and plummet weight and thermometer) the following:

a) Depths.
b) Underwater holes and hollows.
c) Water temperatures.
d) Weed beds.
e) Sunken obstacles/fish cover.
f) Approximate wind speeds (strong, medium, light etc.) and direction.
g) Natural food sources (overhanging trees, bushes, in-flowing streams etc.).
h) Natural food types.
i) Natural cover for *you* to hide behind.
j) Baits most often used by anglers (with which fish will be most familiar) listed in probable order of popularity with anglers *and* fish.

Think big
For big fish use:

1. Big bait.
2. Big, *sharp* hook.
3. Strong tackle, in perfect condition.

*** TIPS ***
a) Each season, concentrate on catching big fish of one particular species.
b) Join, or set up, a specimen (big fish) hunter's club in your locality. The exchange of information, help, encouragement and advice is invaluable.
c) Fish when few people are likely to be about. The presence of noisy humans scares away shy big fish.
d) Be prepared to fish at whatever "unsocial" hours big fish feed (water rules permitting).
e) Fish as close to the bank and your landing net as possible. The nearer your net to the big fish, the less chance the fish has to escape.
f) Expect to spend days and/or nights at the waterside without catching fish.
g) When night fishing, fish "blind"; use no light (except for *occasional* safety reasons); make no sound. Listen, touch and feel. Close your eyes and concentrate instincts and

senses you didn't know you have. Learn to "see" in the world
of the blind – it's a fascinating and useful accomplishment
once achieved!

h) Be inventive, look out for new ideas, tackle and methods
to adapt to *your* requirements.

i) Aim to learn something new each trip.

j) Don't spend all your time reading about fishing; get out
there and do it!

22

RIGHT WAY TO KEEP RECORDS

As soon as you get home from fishing; have cleaned, dried, packed and put away your tackle – record the outing's events.

We learn from mistakes and success. Our records jog the memory, making bigger and better catches of fish possible in the future.

Your records should be a joy to read; store valuable information; build your knowledge and understanding of fish, fishing, wild life and natural surroundings.

Put as much information as possible in your records.

Take pride in presentation. Others might like to read and learn from your records. And one day you may have them published!

Style choice
The type of record you keep suggests the style of recording. For instance, should you want to keep brief records, you can make notes on plain postcards – stored in a plastic or cardboard box; or write in an inexpensive, paper-covered exercise book.

For posh, permanent records, use a large, hard-covered notebook with lined or blank pages; or a ring binder and loose-leaf file paper.

Design
Organise the layout of your records so important information is sensibly arranged and easily found.

Things to include
Note all details you think might be useful to remember next time you go fishing. Anything that could help you catch more and bigger fish. If you have time, record interesting sights and sketch or paint pretty flowers and memorable

scenes. Keen photographers add snaps of places visited and fish caught (see page 67).

Make the effort and turn your fishing knowledge and memories into special records you are pleased to read and proud to show.

DATE	PLACE	WEATHER AND WATER	BAIT AND METHOD	FISH CAUGHT	BEST FISH	NOTES
4th JULY	MILL POND	Warmish and bright. Light breeze from South West.	Big earth worm legered on pond bottom. Size 8 hook.	2 Tench (7.30 – 7.45am)	Tench. About 1kg (2½ lbs)	No groundbait used this trip. Fish started feeding about 7am. and stopped around 9 am.
		Water high and muddy after yesterday's rain.	2 maggots float fished about 305mm (12 inches) below water surface. Size 14 hook.	10 Roach Perch (8.30 – 9.00am.)		Saw someone catch a big eel on cheese cube —English cheddar! Spotted moorhen with three young. Pond skaters active among flowering starwort.

55. Record sheet.

23

KEY TO FISHY
WORDS

We find fishy words whenever we read about fishing or listen to fishermen. The meaning of some words is clear, but a few fishy words may be unfamiliar to us, and cannot always be found in dictionaries.

When we talk fishing to friends, we should try and choose ordinary, easily understood words to say what we mean. Made-up "fishy" words are frequently unnecessary and make fishing seem complicated. Successful fishing for sport is simple and fun!

Here is your key to the meaning of a selection of commonly used fishy words.

Bird's nest: Mess of line tangled around your reel. Careful, controlled casting prevents "birds' nests".

Bottom fishing: Fishing your bait near or on ground beneath the water – at the water's bottom (see "Float fishing" Ch 14, and "Legering" Ch 15).

Brace of fish: You've caught a "brace" of fish when you have *two*. "Brace" normally refers to pairs of the same species of game fish (salmon or trout) caught.

Cock fish: Male fish – usually used in reference to male salmon.

Creel: Not common now, but the once traditional large woven-cane angler's basket; stored tackle and provided a comfortable waterside seat.

Creeper: Larva of the stone-fly.

Dapping: Skilful dangling of real insect or artificial fly on water surface in "natural" bobbing motion.

Dead bait: Dead fish fished as bait for predatory fish, particularly pike, zander and eels.

Evening rise: The customary summer's evening rise of trout to feed on hatching flies.

Foul hooked: An unfairly caught fish not hooked in the mouth. "Foul hooked" fish are accidentally hooked in body or fin when winding back line. Foul hooked big fish can't count as record breakers.

Fry: No, not fish and chips. Tiny, recently hatched fish are "fry".

Gaff: Sharp metal hook on long handle used for "gaffing" large fish (mainly salmon) through jaw for easier landing.

Gag: Device for holding open securely jaws of pike while hook is safely removed.

Gentles: Maggots.

Gozzers: Home-bred maggots.

Hackle: Bushy "collar" of fibres below hook eye of artificial fly.

Jokers: Tiny bloodworms, larvae of the midge fly.

Lee shore: When stillwater fishing, the bank that the wind blows towards is the "lee shore"; the bank the wind blows from is the "windward shore".

Minnow: Small fish found mainly in gravel or sandy bottomed streams.

Pinkie: A small maggot dyed partly pink. "Pinkies" are popular with some anglers and a few fish.

Playing a fish: Art of giving and recovering line, combined with delicate movement of the rod, to tire and land a hooked fish.

Priest: Small, heavy cosh for hitting at the base of the head, and instantly killing, game fish (salmon and trout).

Pumping a fish: Lowering your rod; re-winding slack line; then raising the rod to apply pressure to tire a hooked fish; then lowering your rod and reeling-in more line. "Pumping" continues until you've landed the fish.

Put-and-take fisheries: Waters where owners restock with trout to replace those caught and taken home by anglers, to ensure a constant number of trout available to fishers.

Shot: Weights. Originally, lead shotgun pellets, or lead pistol balls (bullets). The first fishing weights were literally gun "shot".

Spate: Raised water level in river or stream following heavy rainfall. The often muddy ("coloured") water is said to be "in spate".

Squatts: Tiny maggots used in groundbait or for "feeding" (see Ch 12).

Stock pond: Pond where fish are bred to suitable "stocking" size before being transferred to club, syndicate, public or private waters.

Striking: Action of tightening line to drive hook home in fish's mouth.

Swim: Area of water likely to hold fish. You choose to fish a particular stretch of water or "swim".

Terminal tackle: The arrangement of weights (if any) and hook bait on the line fished beneath your float (if any). Essentially, your method of fishing and presentation of the end ("terminal") part of your tackle in the water.

Test curve: Manufacturer's guide to the "stiffness" of a fishing rod. Rods are tested for stiffness of action by suspending a weight from reel-line threaded through the rod rings. The weight which bends the rod tip and end section through 90° is the test curve weight.

A rod with a test curve in the region of 679 g to 1.1 Kg (1½ lbs to 2½ lbs) is adequate for general purpose fishing.

The heavier the "test curve" weight, the stiffer and stronger the rod; but the less sensitive its action.

24

UP-TO-THE-MINUTE
ANGLING INFORMATION

Fishing facts change fast in the space age.

Angling for accurate details may demand skills and patience you normally reserve for hooking fish.

Rather than give information which could soon be outdated, here are suggested ways to pinpoint up-to-the-minute 100% accurate facts about fishing.

General
Fishing tackle shops
Our friendly, helpful specialist tackle dealers know, or can find out, everything you want to discover about: baits, by-laws, clubs, fish, licences, permits and rules, tackle, waters and water authorities.

Repay *your* tackle dealer for expert help – *buy* tackle and baits from him. If he can't make a living and closes down – *you* will suffer!

Public library
Your local reference library stocks fact-packed fishing directories and handbooks. Any books not stocked can be quickly obtained for you.

The library probably displays or has filed, details of local fishing clubs and any evening classes offering practical instruction in casting and fishing technique.

Media
Latest developments in fishing are fully covered by the media: weekly angling newspapers and monthly magazines; tackle catalogues – available from dealers and by post from tackle manufacturers (advertised in angling newspapers and magazines); local radio and TV programmes, and regular columns in some national and local newspapers.

Specific
Anglers' Co-operative Association
Please join the A.C.A. The Association fights water pollution for us and needs *your* support. Find the address in angling newspapers, magazines or from your tackle dealer, or local public library.

Baits
Some baits, notably maggots and hempseed, are banned on certain waters. Check *by-laws* and fishing *permits* for details.

By-laws
These are local laws, varying from place to place, that apply to fishing local waters. Break a by-law and you could find yourself in court; fined and your tackle confiscated.

By-laws are usually listed on the backs of rod licences, available from your tackle dealer, or by post from your area water authority. Check with your *tackle dealer* or *public library* for details.

Close season
In most parts of England and Wales (there are exceptions) NO fishing for *coarse fish* (see page 10) is allowed between March 15th and June 15th inclusive. The idea of a "close season", is to give fish time to breed and recover strength between one fishing season and the next.

Trout
The *close season* for brown trout, in most parts of England and Wales, is from 1st October to the last day of February, inclusive.

Scotland
In Scotland close seasons vary from one water to another and should be checked with local tackle dealers or the *Scottish Tourist Board* ('phone directory enquiries, or 'phone or visit your local public reference library for address and telephone number of the Scottish Tourist Board).

Ireland
Check with the appropriate Tourist Office, as above.

Permits

A permit to fish a particular water is *normally* required *in addition* to an area water authority rod licence, before the water can legally be fished.

Permits valid for one day; one week, or one year are sold by tackle dealers and/or clubs, syndicates or private owners.

Check with local tackle dealers or public reference library.

Don't dodge

Please don't break the law by fishing without the correct rod licence and permit. Money we pay for rod licence and water permits goes towards valuable repair, restocking and improvement work on *our* waters.

25

JOIN THE CLUB

Your local fishing club needs you. And you gain huge benefits from club membership.

Finding your club
Get your local club membership secretary's telephone number and address from:

a) Your nearest fishing tackle dealer.
b) Local telephone directory.
c) The public library.

It's best to 'phone the secretary to find when and where the club meets. Some popular clubs have a membership waiting list; others immediately welcome new members.

Most clubs enjoy a membership ranging widely in age, experience and knowledge; have a junior and beginner's section; give friendly and helpful instruction to expert level, and offer many splendid opportunities and advantages to members.

There is usually a small membership fee to cover running costs. In return the club offers you some, if not all the following:

Tackle Making: hints and help building rods from kits; also making and maintaining other items of equipment.
Competitions: your chance to win cups, trophies, fame and fortune, and maybe a place in your country's national fishing team!
Discounts: sizeable reductions in the normal price of selected tackle and books.
Fishing: on stretches of water well stocked with good fish and owned or leased by the club.
Holidays: cut price fishing holidays in the U.K. and abroad.
Instruction: friendly talks and practical advice from experienced club members and guest speakers; films, slides, videos; assistance and encouragement at the waterside.

Insurance: inexpensive policies to cover cost of equipment damaged or stolen.
Repairs: tools and help required for tackle repairs.
Social evenings: fun get-togethers for you and your family, with disco-dances, games, quizzes and prizes.
Transport: arranged to waters by coach or car to save you money and help members without their own transport.
Trips: exchange day visits to other clubs' waters – to try their fishing.

Your club needs you!
To survive and prosper, your club needs YOUR enthusiastic help.
  Help by becoming an active member and joining with:

1. Keeping the club water and bankside clean and tidy.
2. Making sure the fish are strong and healthy.
3. Assisting your club's voluntary efforts to clear local polluted water, and collecting money for club and national funds to help fight industrial pollution currently killing water life across the U.K.
4. Teaching others to make manners matter at the waterside and behave in a thoughtful, responsible way.
  Clubs are the heart of our sport. Join and help your club fight for our freedom to fish in unpolluted waters.
  You are never alone when you belong to a club!

INDEX

Other Right Way titles of interest to the fisherman

BEGIN FISHING THE RIGHT WAY

Ian Ball teaches you how to catch big fish from both freshwater and sea. With descriptions of the plants and creatures you will see while fishing and with hints on how to develop your angling skills, this book shows how, on a modest budget, all of us can enjoy this great outdoor sport.

THE KNOT BOOK

Do you fumble tying a humble parcel, stare blankly at the end of a tow-rope or wonder why your shoelaces constantly need re-tying? Could you sling a load on a hook, tighten a tarpaulin properly, bind a leaky hose or tether a horse? Geoffrey Budworth shows how to apply the right knot – secure and strong enough for the job. Such skill is not only immensely satisfying, but can be essential to the safety and enjoyment of leisure pursuits such as climbing, sailing and fishing; in rescue, life can depend on it.

In the same series

Uniform with this book

RIGHT WAY
PUBLISHING POLICY

HOW WE SELECT TITLES
RIGHT WAY consider carefully every deserving manuscript. Where an author is an authority on his subject but an inexperienced writer, we provide first-class editorial help. The standards we set make sure that every **RIGHT WAY** book is practical, easy to understand, concise, informative and delightful to read. Our specialist artists are skilled at creating simple illustrations which augment the text wherever necessary.

CONSISTENT QUALITY
At every reprint our books are updated where appropriate, giving our authors the opportunity to include new information.

FAST DELIVERY
We sell **RIGHT WAY** books to the best bookshops throughout the world. It may be that your bookseller has run out of stock of a particular title. If so, he can order more from us at any time – we have a fine reputation for "same day" despatch, and we supply any order, however small (even a single copy), to any bookseller who has an account with us. We prefer you to buy from your bookseller, as this reminds him of the strong underlying public demand for **RIGHT WAY** books. Readers who live in remote places, or who are housebound, or whose local bookseller is unco-operative, can order direct from us by post.

FREE
If you would like an up-to-date list of all **RIGHT WAY** titles currently available, please send a stamped self-addressed envelope to
ELLIOT RIGHT WAY BOOKS,
KINGSWOOD, SURREY, KT2O 6TD, U.K.